The War on Drugs—
The Worst Addiction
of All

The War on Drugs— The Worst Addiction of All

By
Max Hartstein

Writer's Showcase
New York Lincoln Shanghai

The War on Drugs—The Worst Addiction of All

Writer's Showcase
an imprint of iUniverse, Inc.

For information address:
iUniverse, Inc.
2021 Pine Lake Road, Suite 100
Lincoln, NE 68512
www.iuniverse.com

A Twenty-Fifth Century Ensemble Production

ISBN: 0-595-24700-8

Printed in the United States of America

Contents

Acknowledgements

I wish to express my deepest gratitude to the following people for their invaluable contributions to the creation of this book.

To Craig Somers for his marvelous photo
For the cover of this book and my portrait

To Jean Hanamoto for her beautiful marijuana photographs

To Vicki Lee for her invaluable research
And computer craftsmanship

Mary Mastropaolo for the use of her
Crucifix on the front cover

And to my Mother, Frances Hartstein

Without their generous help and support this project could never have been completed

Introduction

I am now seventy-three years old and like most of you I have lived in a society that accepts the government's draconian prohibition laws. The latest of these support the "War on Drugs", as a normal part of life. Our government's tendency to impose repressive and ineffective prohibition laws appeared to end with the repeal of the Volsed Act (alcohol prohibition) in 1932, but it surfaced again two years later, merely changing its target from alcohol to marijuana.

The political arena and the justice system, by their creation and enforcement of these laws, and the media, with their unremitting wave of propaganda, have generated and reinforced an acceptance of these laws by the general public. The result is a massive worldwide brainwashing. The enforcement of these unconstitutional laws and the waging of this insane war have escalated into a frenzy of persecution that is the contemporary moral equivalent of the Spanish Inquisition.

This book shows the truly evil nature of prohibition laws and the real reason they have lasted so long, done so much damage, and are still being endured. It also exposes the war on drugs as a taxpayer subsidized benefit to organized crime. When the responsible people of middle-class America come to their senses, they will abolish these laws and end the devastating, cannibalistic culture they have created and continue to nurture. When that happens, we will have taken a major step toward reclaiming our God-given and Constitutional right to "…life, liberty, and the pursuit of happiness."

1

What is this War on Drugs all About?

I am writing because I care about our country and our Constitutional freedoms in general. I want to show you how the War on Drugs actually does just the opposite of what it purports to do. I am something of an authority on this war, authority borne of experience on the streets of this country. To do so, I have to go back to the foundation of our great country, the Constitution. I will show how our Constitution attempts to establish security, stability, and enduring continuity by guaranteeing freedom and peace, both personal and social, to every citizen, conditions necessary for free enterprise and the free market to thrive.

Let us begin by looking at our local and national governments as the major role models for all of our citizens, adults and children alike. We must look at our government as a role model for the rest of the world, individuals and governments alike. Because we are now the sole remaining superpower in the world, we must set the standard for morality.

We don't have to be perfect, but we must move in the right direction, towards freedom and away from despotic control. How we conduct ourselves will influence all emerging democracies. We will be forging internal and external values, both public and private, between nations, between individuals in our society from friends and acquaintances to families, from workers and unions to bosses and management, between children and parents, and between buyers and sellers.

We know our country was born in an explosion of idealism. People such as Thomas Paine, George Washington, James Madison, Benjamin Franklin, Thomas Jefferson, and the First Constitutional Congress created an historic and singular framework for the future. This framework is found in the wording of the Preamble to the Constitution and the Declaration of Independence; the checks and balances on the powers of the three branches of the Federal government; and the Bill of Rights, the first ten amendments to the Constitution.

Unfortunately, the tradition of "doublespeak" was also put into practice from the very birth of our great and beloved country. So we find our Constitution, this giant step towards personal human freedom, accompanied by a general acceptance of human bondage and outright slavery. We affirmed the sanctity of private property and at the same time witnessed the theft by force and violence of the traditional homelands of the Native American nations.

So we must recognize that a cruel and callous form of hypocrisy tempered the idealism of our founding fathers. It was under these conditions that this powerful nation was created. Now, more than two hundred years after its founding, we find ourselves still struggling, with only limited success, to live up to the lofty, humane ideals of our great Constitution. As the supreme example of authority, our government has led and misled the people since its inception.

To focus attention on the highest goals of our Constitution, I will discuss some of our contemporary problems including the apparent breakdown of our society. These include disintegration of family values and relationships, the spread of crime, drug addiction, alcoholism, tobacco addiction, personal degradation and desperation, and isolation. I will also discuss how the War on Drugs creates the crime it seeks so diligently to overcome.

Our government, because it is legally elected, is a primary influence on all of our lives and our concepts of morality. We must realize that what it does and says creates the overall conditions by which we, as individuals, relate to each other. When a President, such as Richard Nixon, lies and cheats on and about the rules of legal conduct and yet avoids any punishment for his misdeeds, then the average citizen may well conclude that lying and cheating are okay.

Another President said he knew nothing about a policy of lying and cheating, of saying one thing and doing another, such as in Iran-Gate. In that instance, our President said, "We won't do business with terrorists." He then proceeded to sell the same terrorists weapons of war in a deal for hostages. This President then took the money made from this deal and financed violent and ruthless counterrevolutionary terrorists that murdered, raped, pillaged, and massacred their own country's men, women, and children. This policy sent out a message utterly contrary to any form of civilized morality.

We watched on television as our elected President, John F. Kennedy, was gunned down in Dallas. Later, we saw his younger brother Bobby killed at the very moment he seemed to be rising in his primary bid for nomination as the Presidential candidate of the Democratic Party. We have seen our great African American leaders, men such as Martin Luther King, Medgar Evers, and Malcolm X, gunned down one after another.

How can we expect the chronically, desperately poor citizens of our inner cities to renounce violence? We only notice them when they riot. America has a long history of achieving its goals, not by democratic means, but by lies, murder, assassination, and sometimes even massacres, such as those committed by our tax-financed Contra armies and others in South and Central America. How can anyone expect that the pattern set by the ruling class of this society and expressed through our governmental policies, both foreign and domestic, not to be acted out by the most desperately poor and undereducated element of our society? The masses may be kept in ignorance, but they are not stupid! When they see 25 cents worth of lead overcoming millions of votes and the huge financial campaigns needed to achieve a political victory at the polls, what are they supposed to think?

Just imagine, if you will, what our government, and our society, our world, and our lives would be like today if those tragic assassinations had not occurred? If we had not escalated the war in Vietnam, but ended it instead, thereby avoiding the loss of a generation to demoralization, drugs, alcohol, and/or death in battle, along with the massive debt built up in the process of ruining a country and losing a war. Imagine what the world would be like now if our foreign policy had not included destabilizing Chile and failing to prevent the assassination of the legally elected President, Salvadore Allende. If in Africa we had not caused Patrice Lumumba to be assassinated, or if we had not financed and trained the South and Central American Death squads, what would the world be like? Can we really claim any lasting benefit from this murderous past? If so, why are we in so much financial and correspondingly social and moral distress right now?

We were told that these draconian moves were necessary to keep our economy and social structure running smoothly. Did they do that? Who can answer yes? The workers or middle-class businesses of today certainly will not! This is the source of the brains and muscle our country runs on and it cannot survive without stable and morally responsible government. After such continuous and widespread use of violence for so many years as a political tool, how can we expect these abuses of governmental power not to have a negative effect on our society? When in the history of the human race has this been true?

Historically, just the opposite is true. When a government uses violence as a tool to gain power over others, the society at large is influenced to use violence as a personal tool to gain power over others. "Monkey see, monkey do." The influence of government is more pronounced and even stronger than that of the media. The media only mimics and falsely portrays this violence. The government's violence is real. The media are led in this direction by the general climate that governmental violence sets in place.

As a natural outgrowth of the government's violent policies, we see all this played out on TV every day and night. Yes, we see it and hear it, but because of governmental and media "doublespeak" we do not recognize it for what it is. Most of us get our ideas of law enforcement from the news or the TV cop stories. This constant diet of TV violence is certainly a contributing factor in a rise in violent crimes, especially in the inner cities. Why this should be a surprise to anyone of normal intelligence is beyond me. What we have here is a natural human process. Our government, like any other role model, teaches us to do as it actually does, not as it says we are to do. Several of our past Presidents have shown us and our children how to cover up, lie, cheat, and pardon misdeeds by refusing to accept responsibility for their actions. These Presidential actions were all in violation of the Constitution that every President must swear to protect when he takes office.

As some of the recently past leaders of our government have done these things, they have taught an indelible lesson in how to say one thing, to pretend to be one thing, when actually doing and being another. This is a lesson in "doublespeak." By this process, our society sets in motion its own destruction. It does so by creating an inherently antisocial personal environment. We cannot protect our language or our freedom by destroying it.

The same is true with our moral principles of humane and caring behavior toward each other. We cannot create a peaceful, just society with the use of murder, torture, prisons, deception, and violence. We cannot educate or create an honest public or private discourse with "doublespeak." This only causes cynicism, denial, demoralization, disbelief, and confusion. These psychological conditions, when imposed on the society by the example of governmental hypocrisy, greatly increase the tendency towards social disintegration, class warfare, acceptance of totalitarianism, and first and foremost, crime and violence. Along with this goes severe stress, which amplifies all these negative effects into the family structure and causes a general loss of morality and a breakdown in family values, social values, the economic and social fabric of our society.

All this is happening before our eyes, and yet we continue to deceive ourselves into believing that the symptoms of our problems are really the causes. We certainly can't solve our problems if we can't see them, recognize them, and consequently do something about them. Treated with nothing but denial they fester until they poison the whole social body.

The basic cause of our social problems is a huge failure of moral leadership from our government and our leaders. Bad policies of both the past and present, bad laws, inhumane law enforcement, withholding or obstructing justice, and the obvious tilt of this social arrangement in favor of the rich and powerful at the expense of the weak, the poor, the helpless and home-less, and working class wage earners in general, these are the root causes of our social problems.

What these policies have done is to enrich a very small upper class while at the same time, creating a second, lower class of poverty-ridden inner-cities and rural poor where the jobless rate reaches 50 percent and in some cases as much as 70 percent. One must ask, how can this be good for our country? Our future? Our economy? We have tried to hide this by herding the most poverty stricken inner-city citizens into giant housing projects, which quickly turn into ghettos. The environment in most of these projects can only be described as bleak, impersonal, dehumanizing, and extremely grim and depressing. They offer no aesthetic relief.

These policies have created a desperately poor under class of mostly young, poorly educated individuals who have little or no possibility of finding a decent job, and who have nothing to do and nothing to lose. Their main sources of relief from this form of legal racist and economic repression seems to be sex and drugs. The main avenue of economic egress is crime. In a social environment like this, selling drugs must appear a preferable alternative to burglary or armed robbery. Now, instead of looking at this abysmal situation and studying what is wrong with it and how to alleviate these serious human errors and bring about a peaceful, stable social environment, we answer with imprisonment, more dehumanization, the death penalty, which is actually only socially approved violence, and a misguided War on Drugs. This "war" is a process of treating a medical problem as if it were a legal problem. It does nothing to decrease crime. In fact, it produces more and more desperate people who are willing to take more chances, who are driven to greater desperation, who become more violent, and who have less hope, less morality, and less concern for their own and others' humanity.

How could this process of joblessness and poverty and the steady removal of our social safety net ever work? It is a process of punishing the poor people who are at the same time being crushed by poverty. Treating a medical, emotional, psychological, economic problem by imposing prohibition only fills our jails to overflowing. It creates a gigantic tax burden that robs all really effective medical, counseling, and job creating solutions to this complex problem. The more we apply this harsh legal process, the worse the problem becomes. How could it be different?

Everything we have learned about the human condition, since the beginning of recorded history, shows us that this process produces, in a majority of human beings, a very negative reaction. This is not a new idea. The idea that people react in kind to the treatment they receive is at the heart of all human behavior. It is "the Golden Rule." After all this time, and all the great teachers from Moses to Jesus, and from Confucius to Mohammed, how is it that we can not understand and apply this one universal truth, when it is staring us directly in the eyes?

The measures we have taken to fight The War on Drugs do just the opposite of what we want, which is less crime. The imposition of prohibition on society only creates more crime and violence. Only those of us who can buy our way out of these conditions can enjoy the fruits of the free enterprise system we cherish so much.

The thought process that creates this massive social distortion, in our minds and in our society, the War on Drugs, acts exactly like a narcotic. The more we pursue it, the worse our problems become. The more we use prohibition the more we think we need it. As we pour more and more public funds into the War on Drugs, the less we have for worthwhile social programs: low income housing, public schools, activity centers for our youth and elders, clinics and counseling programs for drug users, jobs for the inner-cities and for the infrastructure on which our society runs. By these prohibitions, we are continually reinforcing the conditions that are creating crime.

Instead of alleviating these conditions the War on Drugs makes them worse. As it does so it gives the illusion of being more and more necessary. It is the worst addiction of all. Like tobacco and alcohol, The War on Drugs is legal and lethal. But perhaps the worst effect of prohibition is the criminalization of a very large part of the population. By some estimates, as in the case of marijuana, this may be as high as 65 percent. Considering the vast numbers of people who take prescription drugs and are addicted to these drugs, people from ex-First Ladies to the grungiest street junky, the actual figure may be much higher.

Many of these legal drugs can be more harmful than the worst of the illegal ones. Tobacco is said to cause some 400,000 deaths in the United States of America a year, yet it is legal! Tobacco was the most addictive drug I ever experienced, but I do not feel it should be illegal because that will only create a new wave of crime. I don't think there is anything that the upper echelons of organized crime would rather see.

Of course, we've been through alcohol prohibition with the passage of the Volstead Act in 1919, shortly after World War I. At that time our best young men and women; subjected to the horrors of war, sought refuge in the wines and liquors of Europe, and many came home addicted to alcohol. This was also the case after World War II, but after the extended wars in the Far East, near the golden triangle, (Korea and Vietnam), our troops came home addicted to opiates like heroin and morphine.

During World War II the Germans invented "speed" or synthetic cocaine. After every such horrific and deadly encounter we have had in the 20th century, some form of drug use has been adopted by a great many, perhaps a majority, perhaps almost all combatants, to shield themselves from the psychological effects that modern warfare inflicts. Doesn't it seem rather mean spirited to arrest and jail them instead of treating them for the damage that these wars have caused them physically, mentally, and spiritually?

But I digress. To return to the original point, one of the first things President Roosevelt did when he was elected in 1932 was to repeal prohibition of alcohol. Why did he do that when alcohol is so obviously harmful to all who become addicted to it? The main reason was because this law was criminalizing a majority of the population. That condition leads automatically to an ungovernable population with little or no respect for the law in general. Under such conditions, law enforcement, rather than the protector, becomes the enemy.

This unreasonable criminalizing creates a black market for the prohibited substances and leads to vastly inflated prices and profits that become difficult if not impossible to resist, especially in bad economic times. Prohibition was the mother that gave birth to organized crime: high jacking, gang wars, and, not counting the Boston Tea Party, unbridled social violence. Prohibition brought with it police corruption, payoffs and in many areas, control of the legislative and executive branches of government by the most violent and corrupt element in society, organized crime. Organized into large criminal families, professional criminals amassed huge fortunes. Dare we ask who these people were? Along with the various ethnic "Mafias": Italian, Jewish, Irish, and German, it was the corrupt cops, politicians, and their friends and associates. From the inception of our country until the passage of the Volsted Act these various drugs were not illegal and could be purchased in most places, the grocery store, the drug store, the tobacco shop, or liquor store.

When prohibition of alcohol ended, these crime families did not disintegrate; they were too rich, too powerful, and too well entrenched. Drugs were kept illegal and they became the big money product for organized crime. This certainly appears to be a convenient arrangement between the most successful criminal class and a corrupt political system. What we are experiencing today grows directly out of this prohibition "deal" as naturally as the flowers that bloom in the springtime from seeds sown in the fall.

Who, we must ask, benefits from "The War on Drugs"? Clearly, the primary beneficiaries are organized crime, the police, and the jailers, not the citizen who must pay for all the expense of it. The taxpayer must support the jails bloated with small-time dealers and users. We have more people incarcerated than any other country in the world. More than half of these people (56 percent in 1990) are in jail on drug-related arrests. Most are non-violent people jailed for victimless crimes, but they face mandatory long sentences. They crowd the prisons so much that truly violent prisoners get early release to make room for more and more nonviolent prisoners. In just this way, Richard Davis was paroled from prison and was free to kidnap and murder poor little Polly Klaas. In this way, The War on Drugs indirectly caused her death.

The evils of prohibition, although seemingly difficult to identify because of the mass collective brainwashing, are far worse than self abuse with drugs of any kind, the use of which prohibition has so fruitlessly tried to inhibit. As a direct consequence of prohibition, opium is now refined into heroin, and heroin into China White (artificial heroin so strong it is almost impossible to cut it enough for it to be non-lethal). Cocaine has been turned into crack. Home labs make speed and PCP and all of this is out of control.

After 82 years of trying to prohibit drugs, drug use it is now more widespread than ever. There have been much more harmful drugs created to foil the prohibition of the simple, natural drugs people used to use. By making some drugs illegal and confiscating them when they were transported into the country prohibition caused people to refine old drugs and invent new ones, all of which are stronger and more dangerous than the natural original ones.

Truly, the "War on Drugs" is itself a mirrored form of addiction. The more we use it, the more we need it. We take money from schools, from our children, from social safety nets, from all the positive programs to help our citizens and the future of our country at the front end of the problem, and throw it away on the back end of the problem, which only grows worse. This is a true negative syndrome, one which will destroy our economic system, our constitution, and our free society.

If we don't break out of this destructive habit-forming War on Drugs, we will spend until there is nothing left, no nature, no air, no water, no freedom, no economy, only jails and police, criminals and pollution, and, of course, secret double agents, stealing and dealing, killing and causing death. The corruption already engendered by the War on Drugs has engulfed the agencies and agents who attempt to enforce it. Drug enforcement officers like those in New York, Chicago, Los Angeles, and Miami, bust dealers, take their drugs and money, cars and homes, and then these same agents sell the confiscated goods on the street through their own dealer connections and use the drugs themselves. These are not just "rogue cops" or mere exceptions; these police are more the norm and these are the rules of the game. The exception is the "straight" cop. This is an historically proven pattern. It is an exact repeat of alcohol prohibition during the so-called "Roaring Twenties." Now we also have the Vietnamese Mafia, the Korean Mafia, the Chinese Mafia, The Afghanistan terrorist bombers, the executive branch smuggling agents in this and previous administrations, the Panamanian smugglers, the CIA smugglers, all tied to the "Golden Triangle" in the Far East and the Colombian cocaine cartels, all tied together doing business and making fortunes.

Using the taxpayer's money, these criminal elements remove all independent entrepreneurs who would compete with them. In this way, the small-time growers, dealers and users, all wind up in jail and must then be supported by the taxpayer's money in very expensive high tech prisons. We find that prohibition does not inspire respect for law and order either in society at large or in its enforcers. This is an historical fact continually verified by historical statistics. Instead, by demonizing drug users, we have created a very large group of people who can be arrested, robbed, plundered, brutalized, and even murdered, without any outcry. We have created a national victim class just as Hitler did with the European Jews. Now the United States has more people in jail than any other country in the world. Can this be our way to solve the unemployment problem? We have been trying to export this concept worldwide. Is this what our founding fathers, who penned our truly great Constitution, had in mind? I must confess it seems just the opposite to me.

Are these laws, which propose to tell us how we must relax or get high, in accord with the Constitution? Does the Constitution specify what harmful practices we can do to ourselves, using things like tobacco, alcohol, coffee, tea, sugar, and fatty foods? Some can worship with alcohol (wine) while others like the original population of this land, cannot use peyote (a cactus) as part of their religious rituals. Is this freedom of religion? Is this freedom to pursue happiness?

Our constitution is truly great, and it is the main reason why our country is such a desirable place to live. It seems that prohibition violates the very concept, intent, and meaning of the words of our Constitution the greatest document of social interaction ever created by mankind. Had the Soviet Union had the Preamble and the Bill of Rights, it would still be in existence! Now to us in our brainwashed condition the Bill of Rights seems like too much trouble to be allowed.

This circumvention of the Bill of Rights is the very worst effect of our addiction to the War on Drugs. Please bear in mind that the first ten Amendments, the separation of Church and State, and the Preamble to the Constitution combine to make the best statement enumerating human rights that the world has ever seen. Where we go wrong, whenever we have gone wrong as a country, has been, as it is now, when we forsake the universality of these great humane concepts.

Our freedom and our country exist now and came into being in the first place because of these beliefs. THIS IS OUR GREATNESS, not The War on Drugs, or for that matter ANY OTHER WAR that we have been involved in since the original Revolution. Had we gone to the aid of the Spanish Republic in the late 1930s, there would have been no Second World War, and Hitler would have returned to Germany with a defeated army. Six million Jews would have been spared and a gross human blood fest culminating with the dropping of the atom bomb on human beings in Japan would never have had to happen.

The Nazis had their concentration, slave labor, death camps; the Soviets had their gulags; the Chinese have their work and reeducation camps; and we have our correctional institutions. Our so-called rehabilitation centers are all so over-crowded (especially in California) that they are nothing but court-ordered revolving doors for our most dangerous criminal element, while over half of their population serves mandatory long sentences for nonviolent drug offenses. This policy is extremely anti-productive and irresponsible.

If we decriminalized our drug problem and were able to release at least half of our prison population, we could keep the violent offenders off the streets and locked up while we implemented effective and proven medical procedures, along with counseling, to provide real help for the drug-dependent individual. This one step would automatically end the street dealers and turf wars in the inner cities because theirs would no longer be such an extremely profitable occupation. Drugs could be sold by the druggist, in the drug stores as they once were. This activity could be overseen by the Food and Drug Administration and protected by the police. People who develop drug problems could be treated the same way we deal with alcoholism, not arrested! It is just a waste of time and money to do what we now do and, as I have already explained, it only benefits the big time drug dealers and the Drug Enforcement Agency.

The DEA and those supporters of the War on Drugs keep saying they are winning. If that is true, why do we have such overcrowded jails, at such massive expense to our over-burdened, overtaxed society? Why has inner-city violence not abated? Why indeed do we need another 100,000 policemen on our streets? We are winning the War on Drugs the same way we won the Vietnam War, by losing it. The only place we are winning is in the media, the propaganda front. The dealers are winning and the DEA is helping them to win either wittingly or unwittingly and being paid off for their help with drugs, money, sex, real estate, etc. We the citizens, taxpayers are losing, in our schools, and in the social safety net of our competitive economic society, which by its very nature has periodic economic booms and busts.

These cycles are always the hardest on the poor and working class. So it could be truthfully said "The War on Drugs" is misnamed and is actually a war on the poor, the working class, the middle class, and the Constitution of the United States of America. We can't see this because of the brainwashing we have received over the years from the media and those in government who parrot the "get tough on crime" propaganda line while many of them are actually being supported by drug money.

Finally, we are being told that it is too much trouble for the DEA to be bound by the Constitution and the Bill of Rights. They habitually violate the very laws they have sworn to uphold. This condition is inherently corrupt. Most of us are not fooled by this, but we are afraid to exercise our constitutional right to speak out against this form of tyranny. Fear of public, criminal, or legal reprisal keeps most citizens silent. All this corruption, subversion of our free society comes from within not from outside of it, and comes hand in glove with the War on Drugs.

If we really want an end to street crime, drive-by shootings, corruption in politics and law enforcement, over-crowded jails and paroled psychopaths; we must end prohibition and deal with the drug problem as a medical and social problem, not a legal problem. Morality cannot be legislated or imposed by force and violence. Morality can only be influenced by example. If we want a moral society we must have a moral government. This government must be built on the principles and laws of our Constitution. Those principles are spelled out in the Preamble of the Constitution and the Bill of Rights, a safe, just and thereby stable society with freedom of religion, freedom of speech, freedom of association, freedom from persecution by the government, the right to privacy in our homes, the social equality inherent in the realization that all men are created equal, and the right to the individual's pursuit of happiness.

This is not a position that advocates or supports addiction. It means a more effective program of medical and psychological intervention. It means room for violent offenders in our present jails and less criminal violence on our streets and in our homes without the need for more and bigger prisons. It means a gigantic peace dividend that will support our social security, our infrastructure, our schools, and create jobs and low-cost housing, thereby solving the joint problems of homelessness and joblessness.

We have asked the private sector to solve these problems. We have been asking them to do this, for several decades. They can't do it. In order to survive, business must make a profit. There is no profit financially for the private company or individual to build or provide low-cost housing. The government must do it. But it must do it differently from the way it has done it in the past. We must have truly integrated communities, if not all, then at least enough to end the plague of homelessness and inner-city ghettos. The most tragic error of the "Cold War" was the tendency to view capitalism and socialism as opposites, as though we must choose either one or the other. For a just society, we must utilize the best ideas from both these systems. We must see and realize true integration, socially, economically, and morally. This is the only successful direction of society and our only hope.

2

How the War on Drugs Enhances and Supports Addiction

What is addiction? Some psychologists would say that any pleasurable experience is addicting. Try giving up oxygen or water and check out the withdrawal symptoms. In the spirit of TRUE FREEDOM, I think it can be said that any habit that is damaging to your existence, to your health, or to your ability to cope with reality is going to have negative effects not only on your life, but on the lives of those who love you or are in any way dependent on you. These would include your parents, your wife, your children, your relatives, your employer and anyone that is served by the job you are doing. This is still, however, not a definition of addiction. It is a demarcation of the point or line after which intervention is likely to be needed if the drug dependent individual is unable to end the habit on his own. It is the point of intervention that is socially preferable to both society and the individual.

Treating addiction is manifestly more fiscally responsible and more successful than what we are now doing in terms of intervention. Investigation, surveillance, phone tapping, bugging, arresting, incarcerating, trying in court (with, in most cases, a Public Defender), and then jailing a person is a painful and costly process, and it has been proven highly ineffective in stopping the spread of addiction. It is absolutely the most expensive alternative to dealing with the drug problem that we have. At the same time it is overtaxing the legal system, the constitutional system of justice. Prohibition also automatically creates a black market, thereby costing the government billions of dollars in tax revenues that could be collected from the legal sales of these substances. These tax revenues would make possible a far better way of controlling the market for these substances. This is being done for tobacco, an addictive product that is proven to be very deadly.

Now for a realistic definition of addictive drugs: There are certain drugs that, when taken over an extended period of time, cause a physical change in the body of the user that mimics or imposes symptoms of illness when withdrawn. This condition is commonly called physical addiction. Because of the physical and psychological distress of abstaining from this class of drugs, the user finds it extremely difficult to stop using them after steady use for a prolonged period of time. This is what is most usually referred to as addiction in medical circles. Then there is also the condition of psychological addiction.

In real life, however, psychological addiction is a very common addiction that everyone has in some form or another. We become psychologically addicted to the Sunday funny papers, or the evening news broadcast on TV, or television itself, or eating three meals a day, or living with our mate or our family. Certain forms of entertainment, emotional commitment, competition, love, sex, work, or companionship are also psychologically addictive, but it would seem impossible to outlaw such habits. We must therefore concentrate on those substances that are physically addictive.

To outlaw psychological addiction would mean to outlaw human existence. I don't think we mean to do that. Substances that are physically addictive should be regulated in some manner. Taxes, which would support clinics and treatment centers for addicts to kick the habit are a much less expensive alternative to the present system of enforced prohibition.

Such a system could also get effective treatment to the addict without the necessity of waiting for the legal system to play its game out. In other words, an addict should not be forced to have to wait through a trial, and possibly a jail term or a part of it before receiving any treatment. And, of course, in conformance with the corruption inherent in prohibition, all these illegal drugs are readily available in prison. This is made possible by secret societies of individuals connected to both sides of the law who for economic reasons find it impossible to resist participating. This is true for law enforcement as much as for youth in the inner city. We know this is true. Just read the papers. These are the results of the War on Drugs.

Now let us look at the effect on the addict. In almost all cases the addicted individual comes to the point of uncontrollable addiction as the result of some kind of childhood abuse, denial, or neglect. This is an individual who has unmet needs or psychological illness and is in pain. In some cases, addiction is inherited, but it is usually caused or reinforced by something lacking in the childhood experience, the environment, or both. Poverty is the condition most responsible for the kind of painful childhood experiences that help to create such weaknesses or illness in a person's personality.

Another common causative factor in childhood personality defects that transfer to adulthood is not enough stimulating parental contact. This condition can be found in many so-called latch key children. These are children whose parents must both work in order to maintain a secure, middle-class existence.

Ever since the Great Depression of 1929, both parents working has become more and more common to avoid poverty. First came the Depression, then the Second World War, in which most able-bodied men went into the armed forces. This made it necessary for women to work and to leave the care of their children to others, or else to face long daily periods of being left alone. Then the troops came home, and, taking advantage of the GI bill and full employment, there was a period from 1945 through 1959 in which the economy expanded continuously.

During this period, it became possible to raise children at home with only one parent working and, at least for the white population, a period of prosperity long enough to just about raise a family. This, however, did not hold true for minority populations (African American, Latin American, and American Indian). Their chance to join the mainstream of society ended with the end of the Second World War and the return of the veterans to the work force.

From 1960 on there has been a steady decline in the position and buying power of the working and lower middle-class because of slow but steady inflation. Both parents joining the work force simultaneously have accommodated this economic decline. Thus, more and more latch key kids were created. Children ate breakfast at home with either or both of their parents, lunch at school, and returned to an empty house from 3:30 PM until dinnertime.

I think this may be an American phenomenon. Many of these kids feel like they've missed something, feel an extraordinary loneliness and emptiness. There has always been drug addiction throughout the history of mankind but the recent magnification of this problem owes its growth to a twofold circumstance, the double whammy of almost universally neglected children and declining economics coupled with prohibition.

Here is how drug prohibition affects the addict: In the first place, it drives him or her underground. This person must pretend to be straight and deny using drugs. This individual feels that if you can do it and get away with it then there is no problem, that you're winning the game the government is playing. Because of this perception, peers and siblings see a hero instead of a victim. If drugs were decriminalized it would be much easier for an addict to seek treatment. Then, without police intervention, easy access to treatment would increase the cure rate significantly.

The addict would be seen as a victim instead of a hero by those who now are being influenced by their action, their peers. So here again is a major defect in the War on Drugs, it drives the addict underground, thereby making it harder to recognize addiction, reinforcing the negative syndrome of denial and cheating, at least in the mind of the addict, a game to be played with the police. The chances of winning this game are probably better than 50/50.

All these conditions only delay seeking and receiving help until after the addict is apprehended by the authorities. Because of the laws, a junkie only "shoots up" with other junkies, never in front of his family or other non-addicted friends. That means that only others who are also being affected by the drug are present. This creates a more socially acceptable and more normal situation for the accompanying effects of the drug. If most of the people present were not junkies then the effect of the drug on the addict would not seem to be perceived as normal. The non-addicts would most likely be shocked. Non-users could have much more of an influence on the addict than police intervention can exert.

Finally, we must be aware that prohibition only drives the price of illegal drugs upwards to vastly inflated value. It requires no stretching of the imagination to see that radically higher prices automatically mean more crime. In order to meet these higher costs and continue acquiring drugs, the addict, either with a small or nonexistent income, has to participate in selling the drugs or committing other crimes, such as burglaries, muggings, or holdups, to satisfy his habit. In no way is this an attempt to justify that antisocial behavior, but it must be recognized that these crimes could be substantially reduced by decriminalization and medical intervention, rather than the arrest and incarceration of addicts. Other treatment such as counseling and group therapy would also do much more to alleviate the problem.

Now to put this all together, let us here list the various negative effects of prohibition on the individual addict:

1. Prohibition creates and enforces the absolute need for denial.

2. Prohibition drives the addiction syndrome underground, thereby making it more difficult to see the real negative effects.

3. Prohibition drives drug users underground, thus causing treatment to be delayed, and more difficult or impossible to receive.

4. Prohibition, because it makes using drugs illegal, creates a social stigma that makes the user who is already a victim into a demonized monster in the so-called conventional wisdom of all those who have had no experience in this area.

Drug addicts are usually individuals who have been in mental and emotional pain from childhood. They are often persons who are lonely or who feel unaccepted and victimized. These people have found temporary but immediate relief in drugs, but in one stroke prohibition makes all these negative points in the life of an addict much, much worse. It throws fear into the equation, and creates a victim class, a class that can be cruelly exploited and persecuted, sometimes in a most sadistic way.

An example we all know is the case of Rodney King whom the police, unaware that he was high on angel dust, (PCP) almost beat him to death for resisting arrest. Looking at it from this perspective, it is not impossible to see both Mr. King and his attackers as victims of the War on Drugs. Because we have all lived for so many generations (since 1919) under this spell, we have all been brainwashed into accepting prohibition as a requirement of society, and we have failed to see its real effects. These effects are far more insidiously negative than most of us would dare or care to imagine. How else could we so easily justify this evil?

3

Addictive and Non-addictive Drugs
Blurring of this distinction promotes crossover from non-addictive drugs to addictive drugs.

Let us now attempt to categorize these various drugs into two groups: one group for physically addictive drugs and one for non-addictive drugs. True, there is a lot of back and forth about this, but from medical experience and personal observation (which do not conflict) I think we can safely say that these drugs are addictive.

Addictive Drugs

Opium and all its derivatives, which include heroin, morphine, codeine, vicodin, laudalin, and turpinhydrate.

All barbiturates, sleeping pills, "downers," and tranquilizers are physically addictive. Barbiturates used in combination with alcohol have in many instances proved fatal.

The great big-band leader and trombonist Tommy Dorsey died from an overdose of barbiturates and alcohol in a hotel room while he was on the road with his band.

3. "Speed," (uppers): methadrine, methan-phedamine, benzedrine, dexedrine, and cocaine in all their forms are physically addictive.

Methadrine was first made in Germany during the Second World War. It was created by German chemists on the orders of Hitler to replace cocaine, which became difficult for the Nazis to obtain from South America during the war. Synthetic cocaine or "Speed" as it is commonly called is about four times stronger than cocaine and has four times as bad a hangover or downside as regular cocaine. This makes it more addictive by the same degree. Cocaine is a natural stimulant refined from the leaves of the coca bush, which grows in the high mountainous regions of South America.

The after effects of using these drugs are as follows: loss of energy, headache, runny nose, sneezing, loss of appetite, difficulty concentrating, delayed or removed sexual response, acute depression, and sleep loss and/or deprivation, hallucinations, and weight loss. Many synthetic stimulants such as these were and are used in weight-loss programs. Naturally, the stronger the concentration of the drug, the stronger the hangover and thus the increased tendency for addiction.

4. Tobacco, which has a three-step addiction process:

At First, tobacco causes nausea, coughing, and difficulty breathing, but soon the body of the smoker acclimates to tobacco and for a brief time it seems to be relaxing. Tobacco, after a relatively short time of continuous use, creates a desire to smoke more and more of it. In other words, it is addictive. This addiction is potentially lethal and can cause heart attack, stroke, weakened bones, especially in women, lungs filled with tobacco tar that no longer function adequately (emphysema), and cancer of various organs: mouth, nose, brain, throat, lungs, and lower intestine. The medical profession says this addictive drug causes 400,000 tobacco-related deaths in the U.S.A. every year. What war has ever claimed such a human toll?

5. Finally, alcohol, which is second only to tobacco as a killer drug in the United States.

There are many lethal conditions associated with alcohol which include heart disease, kidney failure, liver failure, stomach and intestinal ulcers, diabetes, Hodgkin's disease, palsy, and stroke. Alcohol can also contribute to Alzheimer's disease.

Two Very Dangerous Drugs are Legal

Of these five classes of addictive drugs, by far the worst of them are legal: tobacco and alcohol. All drugs should be regulated and taxed to help finance treatment programs for addicts. As is the case with tobacco and alcohol, none of these drugs should be available to minors. Treatment should be made available to all who seek it voluntarily and treatment should be mandatory for anyone who is having problems. Taxes should be applied to all drug sales, but prices have to be significantly lower than black market prices to drive organized crime out of the drug business.

Licensed pharmacists at local drug stores could handle sales with mandatory registration of the purchase, and the purchaser. After a certain prescribed number of registrations (which would include name, age, address, phone number, social security number, and place of work) has been exceeded, the user would have to take treatment for addiction. This plan would drive organized crime out of the drug business and end street dealing and the violence associated with it.

Decriminalizing and taxing all presently illegal drugs could pay for treatment programs and possibly even generate a profit. This approach is obviously much less expensive than the crude one we have in place now. The War on Drugs is a policy, which doesn't work, and in fact creates and increases drug use and crime, as well as creating so much pain and violence.

As far as is presently known, these are the addictive drugs, unless we include coffee, tea, sugar, and salt and pepper.

Non-Addictive Drugs

Non-addictive drugs, that is drugs that are not physically addictive include marijuana, peyote, psilocybin mushrooms, hashish (a marijuana derivative), refined peyote in powdered form called mescaline, and lysergic acid (LSD). Because it is produced in unregulated laboratories, LSD can be of varying strength and therefore should be regulated according to strength of dosage. It should be taken the first few times only with an experienced guide present to help initiate the first-time user.

None of these drugs have any form of physical withdrawal. To connect them by law (prohibition) to much more harmful ones that are physically addictive and have either harmful side effects or withdrawal symptoms creates confusion and causes crossover from non-addictive to addictive drugs. Of course, alcohol and tobacco, which are both legal, are the most common introductory drugs, and by far the most harmful.

A large part of the confusion about drugs is fostered by the government's varied attitudes about these different drugs. It is an inconsistent and illogical position to have the worst, most harmful drugs legally sold and transported in public while non-addictive and much less harmful drugs are illegal. Classifying non-addictive drugs with addictive drugs and thereby asking the public to assume that there is no difference between these two categories of drugs creates the impression that the government doesn't know what it is talking about.

By this type of false and inappropriate linkage, the War on Drugs fosters the actual crossover from non-addictive to addictive drugs. Here is just another example of the harmful effects of prohibition and double speak. It is possible to over use non-addictive drugs, and under such circumstances, as with anything else, they may be harmful. But they do not leave the user with symptoms that can be cured only by further use. These drugs can be abruptly discontinued with no harmful physical effects, no withdrawal.

Overdosing on Non-Addictive Drugs

The only dangerous non-addictive drug is LSD, which, because of its uncontrolled production and sales, can lead to an overdose. Overdosing on LSD is relatively rare. It is only possible in the beginning use of this drug. After a few "trips", an acid proof ego is developed which takes over and guides the mind in less frightening or harmful ways. Mentally, acid only gives the mind what it really wants. However, without proper guidance or with a troubled mind, young people have been known to commit suicide either consciously or unconsciously.

Some few cases of overdosing in big cities have been recorded. When under the influence of acid, people have attempted, with no success, to fly off of the top of many-storied buildings. Had these few cases been handled with proper guidance, these tragedies would never have occurred. This, however, makes regulation of production, sale, and usage necessary. This is now impossible, but with decriminalization and the Food and Drug Administration, in cooperation with the pharmacist and the pharmaceutical industry, this regulation could be easily attainable. Of course, there would have to be age limitations such as there are for tobacco and alcohol.

Improper Classification of Drugs Causes Confusion

The rest of these drugs: marijuana, peyote, and the so-called psilocybin "magic mushroom" should be decriminalized because they do not cause problems or harm for their users or society. People using the stronger psychedelics such as peyote, mescaline or psilocybin should not operate machinery or drive or fly motorized vehicles. This is not a problem because the effects of these drugs make such activities undesirable.

Linking these categories of drugs (addictive and non-addictive) causes ill-informed or misinformed (mistaken) concepts and conclusions. It only creates confusion about usage, treatment and enforcement. With confusion comes ineffective treatment, improper procedures (medical and social), bad laws, alienation of the addict, alienation of enforcement agents, and big profits for organized crime. The War on Drugs also makes prisons and prison work a big growth industry, the cost of which becomes an economic hardship like a rock tied around society's neck as we try to stay afloat in the stream of life.

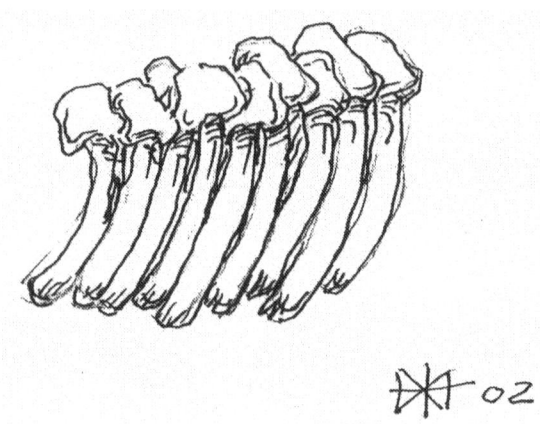

This drawing shows a clump of psylisibon mushrooms. They are usually seen in clumps and I assume they grow in this way, but I have never seen them growing in the natural state. These clumps are stored and preserved by freezing. The effect of these mushrooms is to heighten visual and auditory sensitivity. The user's conciousness of and connectedness to the planetary system is accentuated. The experience is therefore better in the nighttime. In the mountainous area of Mexico where this mushroom grows, it is always a woman who leads the mushroom taking experience. Energy is enhanced and wakefulness is intensified. The effects will last 12 to 24 hours depending on how much is ingested. Users should avoid driving or using alcohol during this experience.

This drawing shows peyote cactus in bloom. The flower has pale pink petals with a golden pollinated stamen. The skin is blue-green with tufts of beige bristles. These bristles or hairs must be removed before eating the cactus. Only the top (button) is effective when eaten. The "meat" is a lighter, brighter green and has a bitter metallic taste. It should be eaten in small bites and taken slowly. If not you may vomit, but then your experience becomes very pleasurable. The effects of this experience is a tingly feeling in the arms and legs, an increase in energy that lasts 6 to 12 hours, depending on how much is ingested. This experience unites you with nature and your atavistic self. Your visual and auditory senses are intensified and you can easily see through rocks and feel the life force in the trees. The user may identify with the Amer-Indians. The leader of this experience is usually male. It is advisable to be in a natural outdoor daytime environment when taking peyote. Users should avoid driving or using alcohol during this experience.

This drawing shows the top of a female marijuana plant. When ripe, it will produce a flower (bud). This young plant is shown early in its growing season. The center of this cluster of leaves is bright green. As the plant gets older and the leaves grow the color darkens. The leaves are usually five-pointed but may have seven or even nine points. These leaves when dried have some effect but if the plant is allowed to mature and produce buds the effect is much more intense. Therefore less is required to produce the maximum effect. This plant may be taken by smoking, eating either raw or baked into cookies, brownies or buns.

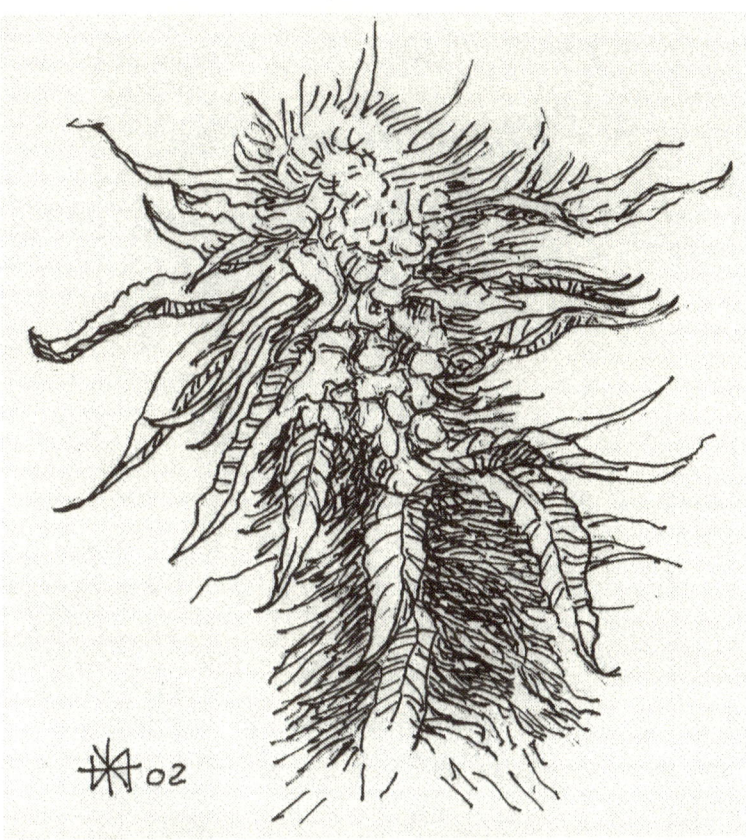

This drawing shows a fully mature seedless flower (bud). This bud is green to light violet in color; it also may be golden or red. It has a distinctive aroma, which slightly resembles a light skunk-like smell. When ripe, and covered with violet hairs the bud is clipped, the leaves are removed, and the flower is hung upside down in a dark, dry storage area. When thoroughly dry, these buds may be stored indefinitely in a tightly sealed container. The effects of smoking these buds are a feeling of lessened gravity, a humorous viewpoint, a feeling of wellness with a relief of anxiety, pain and depression.

4

The War on Drugs: How it changes the Drugs and Affects the User

Smoking opium has never, to the best of my knowledge, caused death. When over used it causes sleep. Eating opium may cause nausea. Only when opium is condensed or concentrated to make it easier to smuggle is it potentially lethal when overdosed. Those forms would include morphine, heroin, synthetic heroin (China White), codeine, and vicodin. Everything but opium, heroin, and China White are presently available with a prescription at the drug store.

All barbiturates, "downers," (sleeping pills) are potentially fatal when overdosed. They also create tolerance in the body of the user and must be increased in dosage to be effective. After prolonged use, sleeping pills make it impossible to fall asleep without using them in greater and greater amounts. They are a common choice for suicide victims. Barbiturates are all produced in laboratories and are by their nature extremely dangerous. Most of the barbiturates are now available at all drug stores with a prescription.

Cocaine when inhaled is rarely fatal. Only when injected (in liquid form) intravenously or smoked in concentrated "crack" form has it ever been fatal. In all its forms it becomes tolerated by the body if used continuously, and it gradually loses its strength. This quality then results in larger and larger doses. As the intake increases the after effects or hangover (as in alcohol) become worse. These symptoms include extreme depression, hallucinations, nervousness, fatigue to the point of exhaustion, sleep deprivation, lack of appetite, high blood pressure, heart trouble, disease of the liver, kidneys, and gums, loss of tooth enamel, and stroke. All this is accompanied by sleep deprivation, which is responsible for much of the worst of these symptoms.

Smaller use on a part-time or recreational basis can, with sufficient sleep and personal discipline, permit extended use with very few side effects. Most users find this method difficult to sustain without eventually escalating to an unacceptable level. This is only possible with cocaine in its powdered form taken through inhalation. In its concentrated "crack" form or injected into the bloodstream it is almost always addictive when used more than a few times. In these forms and also in their synthetic form, these drugs are extremely addictive.

So we see that all the strategies to bring illegal drugs across our borders while keeping them easily transportable have made them smaller, lighter, more concentrated, and much more harmful. Here again, prohibition has created a spin-off industry of secret underground laboratories to refine and concentrate into small packages the original bulkier drugs of opium and coco leaves. All these processes create much stronger and more dangerous forms of these drugs. This is another real effect of the War on Drugs.

5

Non-addictive drugs: Their overall effect on the user.

In the category of non-addictive drugs (drugs that do not create physical dependency), all but one can be found in natural plant form or coming from (refined from) natural plant forms. These drugs have often been called psychedelic drugs. This is because they seem to have the effect in the vast majority of users of strengthening the individual psyche or their psychology of self. They also increase sensitivity to visual and audio stimulation and in most cases both visual and audio amplification is experienced. These effects are only temporary and vanish as the effects of the drugs wear off.

The only one of these drugs that comes exclusively from a laboratory is lysurgic acid or LSD. Because it originates in underground labs, the quality and strength of this drug has been found to have considerable variations. Sometimes acid has been mixed with speed (methamphetamines) or mescalin. This mix is not as safe and has produced undesirable results in some people. These would include paranoia, agitation, anxiety, and nausea. Still, these reactions are actually very rare. However, because there is not a uniform dosage, serious negative side effects have occurred.

Initially, LSD needs to be taken with an experienced guide, and the dosage should be regulated to be small enough not to be overwhelming. After a few "trips", the experience is much easier to manage, and dosage is less important. Normally it takes 24 hours for the effects to wear off completely. During this time sleeping is difficult or impossible. After 24 hours a good night's sleep removes any aftereffects or hangover. In its pure form LSD is the flagship of psychedelics, and it has been credited with many beneficial results. LSD has been effectively used as a cure for alcohol, tobacco, and drug addiction. It has also been used for curing obsessive behavior and other neuroses.

These results can only be attained with the help of an experienced and initiated guide to the acid trip. Naturally, there aren't many trained people like this available since this is an illegal drug. These techniques are not tested or recognized and have thus far not been utilized by the medical profession. Although LSD is the strongest and most dangerous of the psychedelic drugs it is not addictive.

While we are talking about refined powders, which are made in underground laboratories, it is appropriate to consider mescaline and psilocybin. Both these powders are refined from natural plants. Mescaline from peyote cactus and psilocybin from "the magic mushroom." It is however possible to synthesize both these substances. Under the present prohibitive legal system, both these drugs are impossible to control.

Although both these drugs are non-addictive, their use is dangerous because of the lack of supervision or safe medical standards. In Native American cultures the peyote cactus has traditionally been associated with male spirituality, and the psilocybin mushroom has been a female-oriented experience. Using these two organic substances has, however, not been limited to one gender. Men and women have often used both but not together. As in the case of all psychedelic drugs, a guide or leader who is experienced in taking these substances should initiate the first time user. This is very important. With peyote this is almost always a male. With the Mexican Indian tribe that lives where the mushrooms grow in mountainous central Mexico, the leaders are usually females.

Peyote has the amazing quality of uniting your conscious mind with your atavistic ego or your natural self at one with the natural world. In this way it can be a very spiritual experience. Certain links are opened up between the conscious and the subconscious, which facilitate increased visual and audio sensitivity. One can see through rocks and see their composition as natural phenomena (their actual structure). One is able to feel the life force in every living object, be it plant, animal, mineral, or human. In this way, one can feel connected to the Earth in a very similar way to the Native American religion or philosophy. One is lead by this experience to feel the history of America and the Native American experience; to feel like an American "Indian." This is a deep religious experience and should not be denied to anyone, especially those whose religion uses peyote for a sacrament.

Psilocybin mushrooms also unite a part of the subconscious with the conscious and produce a heightened awareness of the planet as part of the planetary system (i.e., the moon, stars, planets life at nighttime). Sometimes subconscious thoughts are released, and these are like hallucinations, one sees these images, as in a movie or a dream. Many times these are inner, hidden fears. Once released, a healing effect usually occurs. One experiences (after getting used to it) an increased sensitivity in all ways, with symptoms such as a tingling or buzzing sensation in the legs, arms, and stomach; the ability to go long periods without eating or sleeping; and at the same time experiencing no loss of energy or concentration. And finally, there comes a certain closeness and understanding of all others, but especially those who are also on the LSD, peyote, or psilocybin trip. As the effects of these substances wear off one feels tired and is able to sleep well and deeply. After 8 hours of sleep the after-effects are minimal or nonexistent.

Finally, let us examine the organic non-addictive substance commonly called marijuana, "weed" or "grass." This is the leaf and flower of the cannabis plant. This substance is used mostly in a dry shredded tobacco like form that is smoked (as you probably already know). To the best of my knowledge there has never been a death from an overdose of "grass" reported or witnessed in the history of the use of this substance. Of course, anything that is smoked contains carbons and particles that can be harmful to the lungs, lips, and throat. Unlike tobacco, the effects of this substance last for several hours so that a few puffs can be sufficient for about three or four hours. This means that far less of it is needed or wanted during the day in daily usage, and therefore far less of it is consumed than tobacco. This fact, plus the absence of any (other) additives, makes this a far less dangerous product to smoke than tobacco. It is also far less harmful than alcohol and of course far less harmful than any of the addictive drugs

Like tobacco, its first time use is more profound than subsequent usage. First-time effects can range from a buzzing or tingling feeling in the head to one that sometimes travels briefly through the whole body. This experience is commonly called a "buzz." Along with this, one experiences a dryness of mouth. Also, there is a feeling of floating or weightlessness; a feeling of joy, of peace, and of humor or the humorous aspect (view) of life, especially your own. If properly initiated into its use, marijuana can enhance the power of concentration on a singular subject or activity. It does so by relieving widespread anxiety and/or worries of the past, present, or future, thus allowing the mind's full concentration on the subject or activity of the present. This trait makes marijuana very helpful in situations of extreme stress. Unless grossly overused, marijuana leaves no unpleasant after-effects other than a slight tiredness. This feeling can be eliminated by two or three more puffs every three to four hours.

Of all the substances spoken of before this one, marijuana is the least harmful and easiest to use. It is easy to recognize and readily reveals its quality like a good wine or cheese by sight and smell. After prolonged usage marijuana becomes a very mild life enhancement similar to tea, coffee, or salt: pleasant, not harmful, but not absolutely necessary for survival. These common condiments and/or substances are where the classification of marijuana should be grouped, not with addictive and deadly drugs like heroin, cocaine, amphetamines, barbiturates, tobacco, and alcohol.

It has been said earlier that linking marijuana usage to hard drugs only creates confusion and thereby crossover to much more dangerous substances. In reality, tobacco and alcohol are the first drugs used by children, and they are the introductory vehicle to other drugs. These drugs are most often the vehicles of destruction. Marijuana is not addictive and is harmless when used in moderation. It should be legal to use and cultivate. Its' many medicinal benefits justify its existence and the widespread use it now enjoys.

Marijuana can take the place of more costly medical procedures such as psychiatry and psychology. It can also replace pharmaceuticals, at least partially, and more rather than less in many cases. It is very easy to self administer and to regulate doses. Its side effects are much mnilder than most of the chemical drugs now used in coping with stress, anxiety, loss of appetite, nausea, sleeplessness, obsessive behavior, arthritic pain, and physical addiction. Marijuana has been found to be beneficial for all the above conditions.

6

Decriminalization—The "Peace Dividend"

We have seen in the last 15 years with the acceleration of prohibition into "The War on Drugs" only an uncontrollable increase in drug use and a correspondingly uncontrollable ballooning of the costs of enforcement and incarceration. This, coupled with the declining tax base, has led to exploding prison populations, impacted justice systems, and overall social neglect. Our schools are vastly understaffed and under funded, and our drug treatment programs have to be abandoned. Because of the drain on our resources for this useless war on drugs, our fire departments are understaffed and our police force is paralyzed and unable to protect citizens. Drugs are out of control. Users probably comprise at least 50 percent of the population, and the illegal drug trade is (if not the largest) then one of the largest segments of our economy. Furthermore, it is an underground economy, so there are no positive social benefits from it. After trying prohibition for 82 years may we ask ourselves this simple question, "Is it working?" Obviously not, (or we're not living in the same world.) Like a true addict we assume that more of the same will cure it. Impossible!

If, however, we were to decriminalize all drugs, these benefits would automatically occur; (1) the black market for underground drug sales would be undersold and driven out of business in a free market manner with little or no violence, thereby automatically ending street sales and violent disputes over sales territory. (2) Drive-by-shootings would disappear, as would turf wars, and drug dealing houses in either the inner city or the suburbs. (3) Licensed pharmacists would handle all sales. Users would be visible. They would register at the pharmacy where they buy their drugs. If they became addicted, treatment could be prescribed. Drugs and drug use would thus be regulated. (4) Treatment programs would be paid for by taxes on these drug sales.

With this program, which I have briefly sketched out, there are obvious financial, health, and moral benefits. If all nonviolent drug offenders were to be released from prison, our penitentiaries would be half empty. There would be no need to spend multibillions on new jails. We would have plenty of room in them for our violent social psychopaths. Addicts would be getting timely and better quality treatment. Health care is a better growth industry than prisons. It has been proven by many studies that drug treatment is far more successful in ending addiction than jail time.

In this way, not only do we not spend billions more, but rather the local drug society makes itself self-supporting and doesn't need as much federal government intervention, provided the state gets to collect and keep the taxes (or at least a large part of them). There would be no need to further employ, at the public trough, corrupt drug enforcement officers who bust the dealers, steal and sell the confiscated drugs themselves, and take payoffs to leave high-ranking crime figures alone. Ending the War on Drugs would automatically restore the ability of the overburdened justice system to deliver justice. A corrupt justice system cannot produce justice.

Then consider the money this saves, money that is now only being wasted and is in fact producing exactly the opposite of what we want, more addiction. This money saved plus money made on taxes, both on the substances and the wages of all those involved in treatment and counseling programs, would go a long way towards solving our present social problems. The money would be there for educational campaigns in the media to stop (young) people from taking drugs before they get started. Wouldn't it be refreshing to get rid of the double speak of "You just say no, while I just say yes." All of this would go a long way towards settling our social problems, our deficit problems, and our health and moral problems. We could finally stop lying to each other and ourselves.

The only way I can find to explain how we can continue to keep this bankrupt policy in force for so long is by brainwashing and our evil fascination with who's doing what, catching them doing it, and then hurting these people even more by putting them in jail and further ruining their lives. These lives are already at risk. We seem to enjoy seeing lonely, sick, hurting people being caught and hurt even more than they are hurting themselves. Pandering to prurient interest may be good press, good entertainment, and good politics, but it is not good mental health or morality.

This approach is definitely not helping the problem of addiction. Medically speaking, it is the same as treating a broken arm by breaking the other one. These people (addicts) are in pain, and we are punishing them for the way they are relieving their pain by creating more pain in their lives instead of helping them to find an alternative and more socially acceptable ways to relieve it. It doesn't work, it hasn't worked, and it will never work.

There are many more positive consequences to decriminalization than just removing the mammoth financial boulder, legal enforcement of The War on Drugs from around the neck of our society. Here are some. If marijuana were legal to grow, use, and sell, we could create a farm product that would save the family farm, that would end the deficit, that would (if legalized) help the Russians to get off vodka and the Orient off opium. This would help to end the massive trade deficit we presently are experiencing with the rest of the world.

If we grew hemp for rope, paper, and clothing fabric; we could find it much easier to spare our diminishing forests by replacing the fiber that wood supplies with the yearly renewable fiber source that hemp supplies with its rapid growth cycle. This, then, could become a completely new industrial process involving three basic categories: paper, rope, and fabric. Of course, it would also be a major farm product. Because it is renewable annually, the drain on our forest could be minimized and a really practical and environmentally sound forest policy could be for once initiated.

Thus, simply by legalizing hemp and cannabis in general, we could end the financial deficit this country is floundering under. We could save the family farm. We could save our forests and by so doing vastly improve our air and water quality. We could bolster our tax resources. We could help to free people from addiction to alcohol, tobacco, and other harmful drugs. We could save billions in taxes now spent on prisons and law enforcement. We could provide workable, medical solutions to our drug problems. We could save our schools by freeing tax revenues now used to apprehend, arrest, prosecute, and jail growers and users of marijuana. We could create many thriving industries and create millions of new jobs; thereby lessening the tax drain unemployment creates while at the same time vastly expanding the base from which we draw our taxes.

These savings could make it much easier and faster to achieve the universal health care that we so desperately need. We will find many medicinal uses for marijuana which will make it possible to alleviate the stranglehold that the pharmaceutical industry now has on our health care system. I am absolutely certain that marijuana will become the next miracle drug.

The bitter pill of prohibition is stuck in the throat of our society and it is strangling our free economy, our free society, and our free political system. All we have to do to save ourselves is spit it out and let nature take over. We will then be able to breathe freely once again the clean air of freedom and brotherhood. Until then, we will not have real freedom, real democracy, real economics or freedom from the fatal confusion of double speak and denial. If we really want to get the government out of our personal lives why not start here?

7

Christianity, Morality, Family Values, Crime, and Punishment

I do not consider myself a Christian. I am a Jew. I am a Macabee. I can trace my genealogy and ancestries directly back to at least 150 years before Christ. Even though I was born a Jew with pure unbroken lineage, it took Adolph Hitler to make me really Jewish. Hitler's bestial policy of exterminating the Jewish race made me realize what it really means to be Jewish. As I'm sure you know, Christ was also a Jew, as were all his disciples and most of the people he spoke or preached to. We know that what he was teaching was found to be profoundly disturbing to the established order, the Rabbis of the local synagogues as well as the Roman ruling class.

We know it was his teaching that eventually caused him to be convicted and crucified. He was, according to scripture, tried by a court of his time and found guilty of heresy five separate times. These trials were considered to be fair by the prevailing standards of those times, much as we consider our courts to be fair today. It was his beliefs that got him in trouble, but even more, it was his decision that he must openly share those beliefs with his peers, i.e. practice free speech. Had he not openly spoken about his differences with establishment Judaism and the Roman occupation of Israel, he would quite possibly have lived out his life never having been convicted and condemned by the ruling establishment to be crucified.

So we see that in his time Jesus was considered a convicted criminal by those in control and was sentenced to death by the standard Roman capital punishment procedure for non-Romans. It must be noted that, at this time in the history of mankind, the Roman roads (which were engineering masterpieces of that period) were lined with crosses much the way our roads are lined with telephone poles. In those ancient days, the authorities were really tough on crime. Not too many big penitentiaries existed then. If you got in serious trouble it was quite likely that you would be crucified. Many thousands of convicted errant citizens were crucified just as Jesus was.

The horrific spectacle of the slow and painful death by this method had two obvious effects. It got rid of troublemakers with very little expense to the state, and it proved itself to be a major intimidation to the masses. It kept them in line and docile under Roman occupational authority. It is understandable that this same fear kept the disciples from removing Jesus from the cross. Now the cross is the symbol of the Christian religion, but what was it then? What was it like to be crucified?

Perhaps it is my Jewish imagination that makes me think these dark thoughts, but imagine with me for a moment what it must have been like for all those countless criminals to be condemned and executed on the cross like Jesus. In those days nails were square. The nails used in crucifixion were about the size of a railroad spike. According to the paintings of Christ's crucifixion (which was undoubtedly only standard Roman procedure) Christ was nailed to the cross as it lay on the ground. Then the cross was lifted and set in a hole prepared for it in advance. It would take several strong Roman soldiers to accomplish this.

After the pain of the square nails would come the even worse pain of jostling the cross as it was raised and plunged into its hole. Your total body weight would now come down directly on the sharp edges of the square nails. Each movement of the cross would be extremely painful, and I imagine there would be quite a lot of shoving, pushing, and jostling as the hole at the foot of the cross was filled with rocks and dirt to stabilize the cross so it would stand by itself.

It could hardly be expected that those battle-hardened Roman soldiers of the occupying army would perform this process as gently as they could. More than likely, these soldiers accomplished their distasteful task as rapidly as possible without any consideration for the comfort of the convicted victim. The cross itself was heavy, and with the added weight of a man on it, quite clumsy and hard to manipulate. The pain of the square spikes digging into live flesh as the cross was lifted and the foot slammed into the hole in the ground prepared for it would have had to be excruciating. When the cross was planted, your whole body weight would then be hanging on those crude square nails, but that would not be the end. The slow, agonizing suffering would just be beginning.

It takes about three or four days for a healthy man to die this way, and in the end death would come as a comfort. In the meantime, the victim hangs upon those terrible nails, naked, shivering with cold at night and burning up slowly from exposure to the sun in the day. For a while there would be bleeding, but after the bleeding, infection starts. During the day and into the night the road was routinely traveled by people, horses, donkeys, camels, and dogs, and was spattered with animal excrement, which dried and became dust to be raised up in clouds by the traffic and then settle into the wounds created by the crucifixion. There would certainly be maggots and flies, wasps and birds feeding on these flesh wounds while the victim remained conscious. All this would create infections of the nastiest and worst kind. The position of the condemned victim with arms held upraised by the nails would be unbearably painful.

This position would cause the infections to travel downward through the blood in the veins of the arms to all the organs and eventually the heart. As the infection slowly spreads so does the pain. Today we call this condition blood poisoning. With both feet nailed together and heels resting on a small slanted wedge, legs slightly bent, one would automatically attempt to push upwards ever so slightly to relieve the pressure of the body weight on the spikes in the hands. This would soon lead to leg cramps and spasms eventually severe enough to rip and tear the muscles and tendons in the upper and lower legs.

We have all seen these kinds of injuries watching professional football on our television sets. When these types of injuries occur, our football heroes are carried or assisted off the playing field wincing and writhing in pain. Sleep might well be difficult or impossible, and all this accompanied by exposure to the elements, dehydration, and starvation. Under these conditions absolutely no healing can take place. The body slips ever so slowly and painfully into unconsciousness and finally death.

Also, imagine the humiliation of being day and night in public view naked and soiling oneself, reeking with the stench of the wounds, the putrefying infections, and all the remaining urine and excrement staining your legs and feet as it exits the body. The relief of death finally comes by suffocation as fluids slowly fill the lungs because of exposure and the raised upward position of the arms. So you would drown in your own mucus while at the same time dying of dehydration.

This horrifying style of enforcing the death penalty did, however, allow the Roman soldiers who enforced it to not have to actually kill the condemned man. As he was nailed to the cross the convict was still in good health, even after the process was completed, and for some few hours thereafter. The soldiers who performed this operation could leave the scene immediately after and a fresh guard or two could be posted to watch the scene and make sure no one tried to intervene before the few hours it would take to bring the condemned man to the point of no return. One or two soldiers would be sufficient for this task. The soldiers in charge of actually enforcing the sentence of crucifixion could then proceed down the road to the next site, with each prisoner dragging his own cross just as Jesus did, a little further to its final destination.

This process of crucifixion with its gruesome and bestial public display created fear, terror, and the ultimate intimidation to the authority of the Roman army of occupation. This was how the Romans brought their version of law and order to occupied territories with very few occupational forces. The actual jobs of government were performed by local individuals selected by the Romans because of their willingness to capitulate to Roman authority. This naturally gave the local Quislings great social privilege. These terrorist tactics (crucifixion) were primarily responsible for what was called "Pax Romano" or translated, "Roman Peace." So it was for a thousand years of the rule of the Roman Empire.

Crucifixion was applied to those who stole from the Roman army garrisons. Usually these were local poor people who stole horses, weapons, or provisions and food. This was a rather common occurrence at the beginning of the Roman occupation. Also crucified were those who were called "blasphemers." These were people who spoke out and agitated against Roman authority or the local administrative establishment, the local bureaucracy of rulers, tax collectors, and religious authorities.

This is what got Jesus in trouble. He quarreled with what was called "Moses Law." Not to be confused with the Ten Commandments. Rather it was the Old Testament concepts of a vengeful God, the concept of "an eye for an eye, a tooth for a tooth", or inflicting an equal vengeance on those who did you harm. Jesus took direct issue with this concept and said instead, "Love your enemy." "Turn the other cheek." and "Love thy neighbor as thyself." He said that God was a loving, forgiving, and accepting God. These thoughts directly contradicted the established religious concepts of his time. He quarreled with the claim of exclusive relationship with God that the Rabbis claimed for themselves and for all faithful Jews.

In his Sermon on the Mount, Jesus taught that all humans were the children of God. He preached openly to large crowds of Jews and Gentiles. He told them that the right way to pray was in private, secretly, "in a closet", and not openly in front of the congregation in the synagogue. Jesus had harsh criticism for the Pharisees, who were the leaders of the Jewish congregation and for the Publicans who were the local administration authorities. He said they, the leaders, the first, would be, the last, in God's kingdom, and those who served the last would be the first. He told of the one wandering sheep out of a herd of one hundred, receiving more care and notice from God (the good shepherd) than all the other ninety-nine who did not stray.

He complained of the bankers' practice of loaning money only to those who could pay them back. He advocated loaning to the poor and impoverished and not expecting to be paid back. He criticized those who publicly, and with much recognition, gave alms to the poor and he urged all donors to do so in private without any acknowledgement. He criticized the haughty arrogance of the ruling class, both Roman and Jewish. He condemned the spiritual leaders and contemporary role models for not only failing God and losing their own entry into Paradise but, more importantly, for leading their followers away from the truth (Double Speak) and thus denying those, who followed them, their own salvation.

He was speaking out against his contemporary culture, which was brought by the Roman occupation. This was an event, which occurred only a few generations past, before the time of his birth to Mary and Joseph. He was successfully destroying the Roman brainwashing, *Pax Romano*, which held sway by terror, corruption, false prophets, and economic exploitation. He overturned the bankers' and merchants' tables in the synagogues and drove them out of the temple into the Street!

To my knowledge, this was the first call in history to separate church and state. More than anything else, this infuriated the bankers, merchants, Rabbis, and Pharisees, who were undoubtedly making a more than generous income skimming off this action. After all, this was the religious money cow of his time. He told the parable of "The Prodigal Son" who sinned but repented and returned to his father, bringing such joy that a feast was thrown. This caused great jealousy in his dutiful brother's heart. By this parable he troubled all those whose sanctimonious righteousness gave them false moral authority over others.

Jesus was shredding the intellectual status quo. He was tearing the local mind set (Roman brainwashing) apart and by so doing was brilliantly and nonviolently destroying the authority of the occupying Roman military rule. They had to stop him! He had to be silenced because large numbers of people were being influenced by his courageous dedication to these truths. His was a dedication to the truth of human existence (the human condition). The authorities, unable to make him recant or bow down in five separate trials, demanded that Pontius Pilate the Romans puppet, sentence Jesus to death by crucifixion.

Even though Pilate didn't want to condemn him, he did so because Jesus could not be silenced and was a threat to the Roman occupation and the pro-Roman authorities that Rome installed. After all, the expansion of the Roman Empire was being financed by taxation of the people of the conquered occupied countries. Roman authority could not afford to be compromised. It would mean (as it eventually did) the fall of the Roman Empire. At that time, the Roman Empire consisted of most of the known world. How inconvenient it must have seemed to the local authorities and the Roman Empire who they represented, to have Jesus so easily shatter their control over the populace.

It seems to me that to understand the true meaning of Christ's life and message, we must see it in relation to the political, economic, and philosophical context of his time. To ignore these elements robs the true meaning from Jesus' message and leaves us with not much more than Santa Claus and the Easter Bunny. This is the positive side. On the negative side, we see the betrayal of everything that Jesus Christ lived for and died for. This betrayal continues today and is lead by preachers whose public prayerfulness is carried live on television, radio, and printed media, constantly in direct conflict with the precepts of Sermon on the Mount not to pray in public.

"Religious leaders" of this kind use their own corporate media to promote their own thoughts and attitudes, not those of Jesus. Even when they are directly opposed to the teachings of Christ, these modern Pharisees raise huge sums of money to further their own agenda from the deluded masses they mislead. Of course, we understand the business and financial disadvantages of practicing the banking principles that Jesus advocated in his Sermon on the Mount (no profit).

As I have said earlier, to understand Christ's message we must imagine ourselves traveling backwards in time to Christ's historical environment. The main monotheistic development at that time was Judaism. The moralistic concept was that of the Old Testament, the so-called "Law of Moses." This concept featured a fearsome, jealous God, with little or no qualities of forgiveness, who demanded vengeance through immediate retribution of "an eye for an eye and a tooth for a tooth."

Jesus took exception to this concept and held that instead, God was loving forgiving, and cared for all mankind, saints and sinners alike. Through his parables he even inferred that God was more concerned with sinners who repented than with those who thought they had lived lives of pure unassailable virtue. Jesus continually championed the cause of the poor, the lowly, humble and downtrodden. Jesus said, in the Sermon on the Mount, and several other times that in God's Kingdom, "The last shall be first, and the first shall be last." His life was a living demonstration of those principles.

If we now jump back to contemporary history we see that Gandhi and Martin Luther King have successfully demonstrated these same principles, and we know they work! Today we are treated to the spectacle of the right wing "Christian" fundamentalists who champion a program that is the direct opposite of Jesus' teaching. They advocate removing the social safety net provided by our government through the taxes that the middle working and upper class taxpayers contribute. This social safety net appears to be a successful form of anonymous giving, as Jesus Christ advocated.

These "Christians" plot endlessly to subvert the wall of separation between church and state. Remember, Jesus said to pray in private and that God would answer in private. Self-proclaimed "Christians" who publicly espouse their version of virtue shamelessly on TV betray Jesus' teachings. They call for the increased and expanded use of the death penalty, for longer sentencing for any crime, and life in prison for third time offenders rather than, and at the expense of social programs, the alleviation of poverty, which Jesus Christ called for directly over and over again.

The question naturally arises, why if one doesn't believe in the teachings of Jesus Christ does one call oneself a "Christian?" Is this not the apex of "Double Speak?" And one more question, isn't there today a familiar similarity to the society with which Jesus Christ took issue? Those with whom he struggled were the advocates of the Death Penalty by crucifixion at that time in history. They believed it to be a deterrent to crime, and indeed it was until Christ himself died on the cross. After that fateful terrible error of the Roman Empire and the leaders of occupied Judea, to be crucified, became to believers in Christ an honor no longer to be feared. So, in answer to an earlier question I posed, the cross became a symbol of resistance. The strongest symbol at that time of resistance to worldly authority it was possible to make. Think about it!

Now let's imagine that we can time travel back in history to the very day of Jesus Christ's crucifixion. Imagine that we can take with us certain high-ranking religious figures and politicians, and with them stand at the foot of Jesus' cross. Let us say for the point of illustration that we have with us some of our current State and Federal political leaders and perhaps some of today's popular television multimedia evangelists.

We're all gathered together standing at the foot of the cross, trying to have a last conversation with Christ as he is dying, guarded of course by two well-armed Roman soldiers. And suppose the conversation came around to this year's political campaigns, and finally we are asking Jesus, as he suffers through his last torment before our very eyes, what he thought about the death penalty, or "getting tough on crime", three strikes and your out, or universal health care or government programs financed by income taxes, to help the poor.

What would he think of a tax-supported government program of supposed crime prevention which either wittingly or unwittingly subsidizes the hidden financiers of the illegal drug market and weakens the legal economy to the verge of failure? What would he think of a "justice" system that handles people with the fury of the Spanish Inquisition and jails nonviolent offenders of prohibition laws for extremely long sentences? What would Christ answer?

8

The Drug Trade—A True Story

About twenty years ago in an industrial park in a large warehouse in the California city of San Mateo, drug enforcement agents discovered 22 tons of cocaine. Needless to say, it made all the news media, papers, radio, and TV. According to reports, an unknown person who saw delivery trucks coming and going from this location had tipped off the DEA. Pictures of the location were shown on TV as well as some of the controlled substance found there.

After seeing 22 tons of cocaine on the evening news, all packed in perfectly matching cardboard boxes, one must ask oneself what kind of control the DEA is talking about. Nevertheless, we, the viewers, were treated to the vision of several stacks of cardboard boxes taller than a normal grown man's height. They did not show all the 22 tons but it was a large representative batch. All the boxes were identical, about 10 to 12 inches by maybe 16 to 18 inches and seemed close to 10 inches high. It appeared to be an unlimited supply of cocaine worth millions maybe billions.

The poor guy who rented the warehouse was to the best of my knowledge the only one person ever busted for this gigantic stash. He was obviously a mere lower to mid-level member of a much larger organization. He seemed to have not revealed very much because (again, to the best of my knowledge) not even any truck drivers were arrested. At any rate, it has all been recorded and awaits only your sufficient interest to track it down, in the various forms that the record of this event exists.

At the time, it was claimed to be the largest drug bust in history by the DEA. At that same time, renewed funding for this governmental branch was being discussed in the halls of Congress. Questions for the first time were beginning to arise about the efficacy of the interdiction policy. Large sums of money were going to the Colombian Army to help track down and destroy the big drug labs in Colombia, and the same held true for Peru were large coca plantations also flourished.

It was said by some critics of this policy, that rather than attack the drug labs, the Colombian Army was carrying out a punitive war on the Native Indian movement, a movement to bring justice, land, and political freedom to the native Indians. These critics said that because of the open violence traditionally practiced by the Army on any strong political opposition to the feudal conditions being forced on the poor Indian farmers, a simple matter of resisting in self-defense was considered civil war. Some believed that political repression was the true nature of the Colombian Army's mission, violent repression to suppress the freedom movement of the native peoples of the Andes mountain range by the terrorist tactics of rape, murder, and land seizure.

The Andes are some of the world's highest mountains. They run through Peru and Colombia. This is also where the coca plant has flourished since time immemorial. These native people have chewed coca leaves for countless centuries. This historic tradition has been practiced by these mountain dwellers to help alleviate the effects of the altitude and to give them, energy and at the same time suppress hunger. It also stains and rots their teeth, and dissolves tooth enamel. The dirt-poor farmers that tend the coca bushes are severely exploited (with help from the Army) by the underground labs that extract the cocaine from the coca leaves. Nonetheless this is a crop that for them is sure to sell for a relatively standard price and guarantee them a meager but reliable income from year to year. It is a traditional plant that they have always grown. It is part of their age-old culture, just as peyote and mushrooms are a part of the Native American culture of this continent.

Now may I ask you to consider why was it that after thousands of years of occupation by the Native American indigenous peoples this continent was still a rich garden of paradise, and after only five hundred years of European dominance, this great continent, this garden of paradise, has been reduced to a level of bare subsistence? What I am referring to by that statement is the fact that we must now stop our blatant exploitation of this land and of these people, or we shall be at the point of no ecological return. We are turning this beautiful, bountiful continent, which in its natural state has everything we need, into the Sahara Desert. The Sahara Desert was once a lush river valley with forests and streams and fertile land where people could live. That was two or three millennia before Christ.

But I digress. Back to the biggest bust in the history of the DEA. Let's look at some of the logistics of importing 22 tons of cocaine. How did it get here? We must assume since the black market drug trade is never done on consignment, especially in such large amounts, that a sizeable amount of cash was transported from some-where in the USA to Colombia in one or more suitcases, probably containing several million dollars. Let's investigate this probability a little further. I think we can safely say that to come up with this money in cash without undue notice, one would have to be moving large amounts of money around continually for strictly legitimate reasons. The first conclusion to be drawn from this is that whoever's money was in these suitcases had a lot of money. It must have come from someone who was rich enough and active enough in the busi-ness world that they could move around a few million dollars in cash without drawing too much notice to themselves.

I don't pretend to know how a money transaction like this is done but one can also safely assume that this very wealthy person would not be taking a vacation to South America and leaving his normal activities and responsibilities to carry a suitcase full of his own money to the head of a cocaine cartel in Colombia, at that time probably Pablo Escobar, and then return to the United States shep-herding his 22 ton shipment of cocaine. I hardly think so! Instead this money would be entrusted to someone else. Someone who was implicitly trusted by the millionaire whose money it actually was. Someone who knew that to lose the money or the cocaine would involve him in serious health problems, like death.

Are you with me this far? OK? Now this other person who is the courier or mule, flies to Colombia, as an ordinary citizen or else someone with diplomatic immunity or something else that makes his trip look legitimate, with the suitcase full of cash. He goes to a rendezvous with the head of the drug ring somewhere in Colombia where he or she sees and samples the cocaine. All 22 tons are present and that's got to be somewhere other than in a hotel room. This meeting would have to be at the jungle mountain lab where the cocaine was processed from the coca leaves. The 22 tons would be moved only once from the lab to the point of embarkation. Right there at the manufacturing site, the product was inspected and the money counted. Then the exchange of money for cocaine was made, and the boxes were loaded on trucks, to be transported under the watchful supervision of the courier or the national armed forces of those countries.

This 22 ton cargo would have to be protected in its journey from the lab to the point of embarkation, because it is illegal and some or all could be stolen at any time. It is then unloaded from the trucks onto whatever means of transportation would bring it undetected and undisturbed into the United States. What kind of trucks? Why, most probably, Colombian Army trucks, trucks paid for by the American taxpayer in subsidies for the Colombian Army, the army supposedly fighting the good "War on Drugs."

I'm sure the soldiers involved get something for their efforts: money from us, drugs from the cartel. Their efforts would include, loading and unloading the boxes onto and off the Army trucks, all the while guarding the shipment with weapons and ammunition provided by the U.S. taxpayer as a partial expense of the War on Drugs. I can't imagine any other scenario for getting 22 tons of cocaine in smallish cardboard boxes safely from the lab to the point of debarkation. That means the safe transportation of 22 tons of highly inflated substance was transported and guarded by U.S. taxpayers' money from the lab or production center to the point of debarkation.

Now let's look at how it could have gotten from there to the market or warehouse in San Mateo. There's a lot of space, a lot of borders and a lot of saltwater between Colombia and California. It is inconceivable that 22 tons of cocaine could be transported north across all the various borders by land in trucks. That involves too many pay-offs. Nor could it be brought into our country by thousands of people hiding it in their shoes or socks or taped around their waists. No, those tall stacks of boxes that we saw on our local TV evening news report were probably shipped from Colombia to the U.S. in one shipment. That means either a large cargo airplane or a large ocean-going cargo ship, directly from Colombia to the seaport of San Mateo or a nearby airport.

If shipped by freighter on the sea, the whole shipment would be loaded into huge cargo containers and then into the hold of some international cargo freighter. That means bribing the captain and quite possibly some or all of the crew. That also means losing a few boxes. It is also necessary for one or more armed guards to ensure the safety of the shipment unless it was shipped on an American service vessel (i.e., Navy, Coast Guard). That would also be a good way to get it past Customs at the U.S. port of entry. If the 22 tons were transported by air it would probably be in a large cargo transport airplane, the kind used by the Air Force to transport wartime cargo and/or troops or large shipments of food, hardware, ordinance, and other supplies. Remember Ollie North who said the planes carrying supplies to the Contras didn't come back empty from South America. So there again taxpayers money was being used to ship drugs into the U.S.A.

Now I want you the reader to understand that I have absolutely no knowledge or any real information from first-hand observation, that these imaginings are the real facts, but how else could 22 tons of cocaine be smuggled into the USA? At very best there would have to be a lot of smaller to big payoffs. If the shipment had immunity or some other way of avoiding Customs then there would only have to be one or two bigger payoffs. Of course, the fewer people that knew, the better and safer for the original (big) investor. Don't forget that there's still the courier (the only one who may know the financier's identity) who brought the suitcase and left with the boxes, unless they were shipped back with the US military or some other governmental agency (say for instance the C.I.A.). Was this Ames real job? Oh well, at this point I can only conjecture. With all my imaginative powers in full gear I can't think of too many or any other workable alternatives.

Now if you're still with me, let's try to imagine how the shipment got from wherever it landed to the warehouse, where it remained undisturbed (and was sold from) for an unknown but obviously somewhat extended period of time. Enough time for delivery trucks to come and go and be noticed and finally busted, conveniently at the most politically expedient time for the DEA.

You must remember that, if known about by other underworld groups, this shipment or any other similar contraband could be stolen without any legal recourse. Therefore, a shipment this large has to be guarded completely and continuously from the hidden mountain processing lab to its final destination in the States, unless it is shipped (either knowingly or unknowingly) by some government agency with high security clearance. That would either be a branch of the armed forces or a sensitive or secret government agency, such as the DEA or the CIA.

If that was the case, then plain-clothed government agents could guard the shipment of 22 tons of cocaine. This scenario has been suggested often by many other sources. There is a proven record of uniformed Colombian Army personnel performing as armed escorts of large cocaine shipments from the drug labs in the Colombian mountains to ports of embarkation.

This has created a conspiracy that is very hard to prove. Just as with the Haitian Army which is also rumored to be deeply involved in smuggling drugs into the USA. The compensation to the generals and on down in the local scale of rank is so considerable and the actual legal pressure from their own and our governments so faint that there is little incentive to inform on this action. Drugs and money can be substantial perks. Then, of course, potential whistle blowers keep turning up dead. This is a condition that could be described as an international conspiracy. If so, how can the governmental policy that created this conspiracy be expected to end it? The only provable fact is that there was a bust of 22 tons of cocaine in a San Mateo warehouse.

Whatever happened to the 22 tons of evidence? Was it destroyed? If so, how? If burned, what happened to the public's safety for 100 miles downwind? Folks, could it be that a large part of the taxes we pay to support the War on Drugs is actually used to finance the transportation of illegal dangerous drugs into this country? Remember there's no return on this investment. The drugs are sold on the street for vastly inflated street prices. This is a situation without any hope or intention of ending the scourge of drug addiction. Rather, it thrives and depends on addiction for its very existence. Why indeed would the enforcement agencies seek a solution to this problem when they are in their own way addicted to the addiction of drug law enforcement?

Okay, so in this way, money is being taken from the public school system, from the Social Security system, from the health care system, from the infrastructure, all to support this horrible conspiracy of drug enforcement and drug business. If this isn't happening in front of our eyes, then what is? Why is the suicide rate so high in the enforcement profession? Newsweek (9/20/94) says more cops die from suicide than from gunshots inflicted by criminals. So this is the sad situation that we now have in the so-called "land of the free and home of the brave." Rampant corruption! Poverty! Failed schools with broke or broken school systems. A great health system until you try to use it. Then they'll take everything you've got just before you die, while we suffer in the throes of prolonged illness until death. All coming along with poisoned water, poisoned air, and poisoned food, and more people in prison than any other country except Russia.

Now let's take a quick look at organized crime. Remember that Richard Nixon was elected president in the leadership vacuum created by the Kennedy assassinations. Many think this timely occurrence for Nixon's power ambitions was accomplished by or with the assistance of organized crime. If this is true, then organized crime became the power behind the throne in the oval office just as it was, and still is, in Italy. If this is so, then the American taxpayer is subsidizing organized crime by eliminating its competition from smaller independent actors in the black market, while providing safe transit for their large black market drug shipments. This arrangement gives the hidden leaders of the organized crime syndicates the comfort of knowing that their connections in government will stay with them because of the readily available blackmail of disgrace and jail time, if not assassination.

Nixon, early in his second term, initiated the War on Drugs with a three million dollar contribution to the Mexican government to bust citizens of the USA who lived or were vacationing in Mexico. That gift from the U.S. taxpayer gave birth to countless extortions of US citizens by the Mexican federales. Want more of the same? Just shut your mouth and keep paying for the War on Drugs. Don't think that was the only 22 tons of cocaine shipped to and stored in the USA and sold eventually on the streets of the inner-city ghettos. This must be happening all the time! It is happening all over the USA and all over the world. Drugs are readily available all over the USA and the world. The only way to end this corruption is to end prohibition!

9

A Tragic Personal Experience Caused by the War of Drugs

This story is a very personal one. It's about my own experiences and the tragic death of Bob, a very dear friend. In order to protect everyone involved in this true story, I have changed the names. When I first met Bob, he was a tall, handsome, young blond piano player of obvious Scandinavian ancestry. He had migrated to the west coast from a northern Midwestern state that bordered Canada and the Great Lakes. He spent his childhood and adolescence on a family farm owned and run by his parents. Like a good farm boy he was able to fix his old Volkswagen bug, do carpentry, electric wiring, plumbing, and all necessary maintenance. He was a college graduate, with a grade school teacher's degree. Above all, he was a very good piano player.

We always enjoyed playing together. These good feelings created the inspiration for fiery, yet cohesive maximum freedom within an accepted formal structure, playing together and staying together by a process of spontaneous consensus. When disputes about the music or its performance develop in a band, even the best musicians may have trouble staying together. It's all about attitude; that's half the battle.

Bob's attitude was the greatest. He was helpful, careful not to over-play, but always there. He had a way of being open to change, look-ing for the new, never playing two choruses the exact same way. That quality, plus his deep musical knowledge made him an excit-ing, original, and never boring musical companion. Bob was a mas-ter of the technique of voicing or substitution of alternative chords that allow the maximum number of choices for the soloist. Not every piano player knows how to do this as well as Bob did. The band's main function was to provide the best place for visiting musi-cians to sit in and jam. The stage was open to whoever could play. With Bob, Chuck Thompson on drums, and myself on bass we had a good rhythm section.

Bob was married to a gorgeous, healthy, young blonde farm girl with whom he had grown up. They had met in grade school and become childhood sweethearts. We will call her Ilene. Even after three children, Ilene was still a knockout. She had long blonde hair that hung down to her waist when it wasn't braided. With their three tow-headed children, two boys and a girl each separated by a year, they were a striking model family.

This story took place in the late fifties and early sixties. Bob and I were the same age. We had been born during the Depression, before the atom bomb, before pervasive worldwide pollution, and before the Second World War, when things seemed a lot simpler and less paranoid. Those brief years of our young lives were filled with a kind of hope, peace, and innocence that helped to create a calmer, more positive attitude than may be common today. That attitude, combined with the childhood experience of growing up on a Midwestern farm, made Bob an easygoing, calm, gentle, giving kind of guy. He loved his kids and spent much of his time with them.

When they first came to California, Bob worked in the public school system teaching music and science to fifth and sixth graders. They settled into city life in San Francisco and Bob met and played with local musicians. Eventually, he was able to realize his goal of working full-time as a jazz musician. Ilene also worked part-time as a receptionist in a downtown office. After Bob became a full-time player, he would be with the children in the daytime while Ilene was working, and she would care for the children at night while Bob was working. They lived in an antique house that they were gradually fixing up, carving a beautiful, nostalgic carpenter's delight, from a big city slum dwelling.

Bob's dream of coming to a big city with really good jazz players and working as a full-time musician was being realized. I'm not really sure what Ilene's dream was, but after knowing her for a while, it seemed to me that she was still looking for love. Ilene had an active sense of humor. She was strong, outspoken, but not a compulsive talker. She was a good mother who loved and enjoyed her children. She could type, bartend, waitress, cook, sew, keep a clean house and write poetry which she kept very private. She was a well-rounded and talented person. When I met them, they seemed to have the kind of marriage for which everyone longs.

Bob and I met in a low rent basement jazz club in the North Beach, San Francisco's Italian and artists' community at that time. The club was under an Italian restaurant and grocery store. It had been a much larger "speak easy" during Prohibition. Most of the available space was not being used. Simple plasterboard walls enclosed the long, narrow bar and one row of tables and chairs, with an aisle between them. The place served only beer and wine, along with snacks, coffee, and soft drinks. To add to your confusion, we shall change the club's name and call it the "Jazz Underground." Most of the space of the old "speak easy" was unused, or simply used for storage. There was a rather large band room, entered only from the bandstand at the far end of the room. The band room was furnished with decomposing overstuffed couches and wooden beer cases.

The bar business was owned by two drummers who took turns playing or tending the bar. The somewhat full-time bartender was "Big John" who also served as the bouncer. Big John was an amateur drummer and poet. He was also an alcoholic and not always available to perform his duties. He was a large, dark haired Irishman with, when not too far out, a very lovable disposition and a gift for conversation. These endearing qualities made it easy to overlook his problems with strong drink. Big John was one of the first poets to read with jazz accompaniment at the "Underground."

This was all happening in the late fifties, when Herb Caine coined the term "Beatniks." While we hated the name, we were in the process of defining what he meant by it. To ourselves, we were just jazz musicians, willingly suffering the economic hardships of the artist, rather than the dulling nine to five conformity of the Eisenhower era. Paling around with painters, poets, writers and street philosophers, we thought of ourselves as Bohemians. San Francisco was in cultural ferment, especially in North Beach, which was the center of the action. It was one of the city's best weather neighborhoods. Older retired Italians owned most of North Beach. Chinatown, with its wonderful inexpensive food, was just around the corner.

Rents were low and food was cheap. You could get a really delicious home cooked Italian dinner with soup, salad, antipasto, and a main course with plenty of bread and vegetables and dessert for a buck and a quarter. In Chinatown, it was even cheaper.

Bob Kaufman was reading his poetry on the street in North Beach and because it sometimes contained cursing and other expletives, he was ordered to stop. When he didn't, the police beat him every time they found him out there doing it. The beatings finally ruptured both his eardrums and rendered him deaf, but he never stopped writing or reading in public and later became famous through the publishing of his work.

Nonetheless, these confrontations with the establishment eventually drove the poets, painters, sculptors, and musicians out of North Beach; and when the sons of the elderly or deceased took over, they gentrified the old Barbary Coast, a one block long section of strip joints. Then they brought to North Beach topless dancing and sex clubs. It became a virtual red light district. Of course, all of this was done with the idea (fantasy) of cleaning up the North Beach district. This change was epitomized by the Old Italian haberdashery on the corner of Broadway and Grant that was turned into the topless club in which Carol Doda danced. The club was later to be the site of a strange on-stage murder. A male dancer was crushed under a grand piano that fell on him. Bob Kaufman, whom we mentioned before, was one of the many poets that read with jazz accompaniment at "the Underground." Others included Lawrence Ferlingetti, Bob Briggs, Gregory Courso, and many others such as Ruth Wiess and Nancy Buetti.

Bob, the club owner and piano player and his wife Ilene were very much behind the jazz and poetry movement. Their backing of the process at the Underground gave jazz and poetry a stage in a time when such spaces were very rare or nonexistent. We had one or more poets on stage every Wednesday, largely attributable to Bob and Ilene's support. Many jazz players hated it, and some were very uncooperative, but not at the "Underground."

We did our best to put them in the foreground, in front, featured like vocalists. Many players don't like playing softly and holding back for vocalists either, but that's what you have to do, so they can be heard distinctly. It's even more so for a poet. It was always so frustrating and sad to see a poet forced to shout at the top of his lungs to be heard over the music. Even if heard, the words tend to lose their meaning. Bob was always musically very supportive of the poets.

I had the poet who was reading that Wednesday evening over to my studio apartment in the afternoon and rehearsed with them what they were going to do, working out little arrangements so that they had enough space and we had some too. The poets were always very eager to do this planning and rehearsing, and it made for some very original and sophisticated performances.

I shall digress from the story of Bob and Ilene to explain how it was that I became the house bass player at the Underground. I came off a very unpleasant road tour with a big band. The experience was so stressful that I gave up playing for a while. I went to live with my parents and help my father build his furniture store in San Jose. This was a way out of the stress I was experiencing and not unpleasant, but I missed playing, I missed my friends and the jazz scene. I missed music, so I would spend a weekend evening in San Francisco, catching the big names as they came through, and I usually ended up at the Underground. People were always glad to see me and Bob would insist that I play a set or even just a tune.

Bob was so kind and appreciative that I became a regular weekend player and started practicing again. About the time the store was ready to open, the construction having been completed, Bob asked me to take the job as the house bassist.

My schedule was to play six nights a week, five hours a night from nine until two, and twice on Sunday, three to six and then nine until two. I was thrilled to take the job, even though (for all those long hours) it paid exactly the same as my first steady job ten years before: sixty-five dollars a week. By that time, Bob had bought into the "Underground" and was the third partner. He had a lot of influence at the club, and pulled me right in. I moved back to San Francisco, got a large apartment just around the corner from the Underground where I could paint and walk to work. I shall forever be grateful for Bob's encouragement and sponsorship back into the jazz world.

I remained on the job for eighteen months, the longest, steady, six nights a week club job I've ever had or for that matter, any other employment. But especially in music, coming to work at the same place, same time, same band, night after night, gets really stale. Without Bob's special talent for open playing, his ability to be moved, and the ability to listen and change his mind, I could never have lasted that long.

If there was one thing that Bob proved to be absolutely incorruptible about, it was his concern for the quality and upward advancement of the musical performance on the stage at the Underground. During my eighteen months there, he allowed me to scout young talent new in town so we could use them on our gig before their ability and reputation brought them better offers of more money than we could pay. We used Brew Moore who was well known but had some difficulty holding a job because of his alcoholism. Brew never let us down musically, but after the job he needed a baby-sitter to keep him from harming himself.

Everyone connected with it was giving a major part of their lives to keep the Underground going, especially Bob and Ilene. As I mentioned, I lasted a year and a half until the stress, responsibility, and the slowly declining economy, coupled with the gradually rising inflation and the paltry fixed pay finally got to me. It must have been for similar reasons that Bob and Ilene's marriage broke up. Ilene took the kids and left town to settle in Big Sur with Bob's best friend, a young artist.

The next bit of this drama to unfold was a fire in the Underground that ended its operation, but only temporarily. With the money from the insurance and help from the owner of the property, who was solidly behind the enterprise, they expanded, remodeled, went into debt, hired the manager of the "Jazz Workshop", and tried to go big time. I was asked to return and play in the house rhythm section, which included Melvin Ryan on piano and the late Smiley Winters on drums.

We opened the new "Jazz Underground" with Dexter Gordon. Dex had just been released from prison in Los Angeles (for a drug bust) and was in magnificent shape, tall, slim, healthy and playing marvelously. For me, it was a dream come true. We kept Dex for a month instead of a week and things seemed to be going well. However, after a few months, the massive expenses of the operation and the manager's phone bills bankrupted the club, and it closed the doors after the Ben Webster/Jimmy Witherspoon show.

Bob then followed Ilene to Big Sur and took a position teaching school so he could be near his kids. He also took over the management of a small rustic motel on Highway 1, which is the main road through Big Sur country. The motel, although small and somewhat grungy, had a bar and restaurant that Bob turned into a jazz club on weekends. The club catered to the organic food crowd, serving mostly vegetarian organic meals. He and Ilene were on friendly terms, and Bob renewed the friendship with his artist friend with whom Ilene was now living. Bob was in daily contact with his children, whom he taught in the small rural school they attended.

In Big Sur Bob grew a beard and let his crew cut grow until he looked like a disciple. He seemed to be thriving. He lived in quarters at the motel. His children, Ilene, and her artist lived in the rugged hill country off the main road. If you are at all familiar with Big Sur country, you will know that in many ways this situation was not too far from idyllic.

In my own life progression I had once again left the stress of the music business and retired to a studio in Mexico in a small village high in the mountains in central Mexico, where I sketched and painted. Missing music, I returned to San Jose, California where I resumed playing jazz. My range of jobs expanded to an area just north of San Francisco, through San Jose, Santa Cruz, Carmel, Monterey and Big Sur. About once a month I would drive to Big Sur and play a bit with Bob on the weekend, either sitting in or working as the bassist. After the gig we often hung out at Esholam in the hot mineral baths.

The next big move in my life came as a result of my beautiful 250-year-old solo Italian string bass being stolen out of my car, which was parked on a busy well lit street in North Beach. I was inside Mike's restaurant and pool hall having a bowl of good rich minestrone after my gig at the bar of a local hotel just a few blocks away in downtown San Francisco. It was a job for piano and bass. Shelly Robbins was the pianist. Shelly was handsome, suave, and debonair, with a quick mind and brilliant technique. He knew more tunes than anyone I have ever worked with and he swung. We went to Mike's together that night as we often did. The theft was so well done that even though I was only a few yards away from the scene with a view of my car from where I was sitting, I was unaware that the theft had taken place.

When we finished the soup and returned to my car, I discovered that the small wind wing window in the front door had been broken and was open. The bass was gone. I was devastated. The bass was the best instrument I have ever played and the positions on the fingerboard just right for my hand. That bass was so good it launched me into the upper levels of jazz music. It has proven to be irreplaceable. I wept bitterly for many hours over this bad luck.

Eventually, after a series of inadequate replacements, I went to Europe to find another handmade antique bass, the equal of the one stolen. I believed, as had been told to me, that there were many such instruments still available in Europe. Unfortunately, when I started looking in England, France, and Spain, I was told all the good ones had been bought and taken to the U.S. Nevertheless, I found a fair replacement and had the extremely good fortune to play for a month with Kenny Clark and Bud Powell at the Paris Blue Note.

When I returned to the States, I rented a loft in New York on the Bowery, at the corner of 3rd and Houston. It was the center of the Bowery. Both sides of the street were littered with men, mostly veterans, in all the various stages of drunkenness, from staggering to out cold. I loved my loft, but the action outside became unbearable, and I left the "Apple" in 1963 after President Kennedy's assassination and returned to California.

Back in the sunshine state, I settled in with a piano player and jazz disc jockey. The piano player was a good and generous friend, and a good piano player. He lived on a houseboat in Marin. I started out again on the West Coast and looked up old acquaintances to let them know I was back.

I inquired about Bob and learned that my dear friend Bob had died of an overdose of heroin. His body had been found in his pickup truck on the side of a little used road in the Big Sur Mountains. I was shocked, because to my knowledge Bob had never used hard drugs. As the story unfolded, it turned out that another long-time friend of Bob's, a talented jazz drummer whom I shall call Billy, had just returned from a world tour. With him, he had managed to bring back some extremely strong "horse" from Japan.

This was an underground product for which Japan had been noted. Billy was a heroin addict, a loose living kind of guy and, as is often the case, a who used and misused other people. Apparently, because Billy was acclimated to the potency of this kind of heroin; he presumed that everyone else would be. He had persuaded Bob to try some, and unfortunately, because of Bob's lower tolerance of the drug, Bob overdosed.

Of course, Bob's dabbling with the strong heroin was a tragic mistake for him to make. However, such a medical emergency is not difficult to handle. A saline solution is administered intravenously and can usually bring the victim back from the edge. These people were in a vehicle and could have brought Bob to the emergency treatment facility, but that building also housed the fire department and the local police station for Big Sur. Obviously because of this prohibition, we have come to call the War on Drugs, all those in the car would have been arrested and sent to jail for long prison sentences. Considering that probability, Bob's erstwhile friends tried, I'm sure, to bring him back themselves, and in the process, being unable to do so, waited too long for any treatment to succeed. And so his body was left on the side of the road, yet another victim of the War on Drugs. As we ponder this terrible, unnecessary tragedy, hundreds and eventually thousands of citizens are paying with their lives for the massive blunder of driving drug use underground.

This is just one personal example of what the War on Drugs is really doing to people. It is directly responsible for most of the deaths caused by an overdose of hard drugs. It is directly responsible for the artificially high prices of illegal drugs, making them so highly profitable that the temptation to exploit this black market is irresistible for everyone from the secret financiers down to the lowly street dealers. It is directly responsible for the pervasive corruption of the law enforcement and justice systems that links them to organized crime. It is directly responsible for diverting tax revenues from the social safety net to the giant pork filled prison system. It is directly responsible for eroding our constitutional rights, our once free society, our free market, and our right to the pursuit of happiness. It is directly responsible for so much misery that it simply must be ended and replaced with a more sensible and humane system of control and regulation.

10

The War on Drugs
Who is Winning, Who is losing?

In the movies and on TV, when a serious crime is committed, and there are no witnesses, the police always look for a motive or a person with a motive to commit such a crime. This is also the case in real life. When a crime such as murder is committed, and there is no direct evidence, but rather only circumstantial evidence, law enforcement agencies always try to establish a motive and then link that motive to either a suspect or group of suspects. They then focus their investigation in that direction and almost always, in fiction and quite often in real life, come up with an indictment. The trick is to see who benefits the most from the eventual outcome of the commission of the crime. Naturally the victim loses and there are also associated losses and peripheral damage.

In the spirit of this successful law enforcement procedure, let us investigate who it is that really benefits from the War on Drugs and who it is that loses. Consider cocaine. In the jungle mountain lab where it is produced, it costs $500.00 a pound but will eventually sell on the Street for $100,000.00 or more. What this shows us is an extremely high rate of profit on the black market, a rate that defies the financial laws of supply and demand.

This profit rate, said to be as high as 3000 percent, is only possible because cocaine is prohibited and illegal. If free market competitive pricing were possible, the profit margin would fall precipitously to somewhere around 100 percent, which would lower its profits and price dramatically. What this fact shows us is that the secret high-level financiers and the big dealers of the illegal drug market are making a lot of money buying illegal drugs cheap and selling them dear. These drugs are principally heroin and cocaine because they are condensed and refined to make them much smaller in size and multiplied in strength. For the secret wealthy big-time financier this is simply good business. It increases the profits and makes the smuggling of these products far easier and much less expensive.

Prohibition is a direct price support to the highest and richest element of organized crime. It exists as an unspoken by-product of the War on Drugs, and it is paid for by our taxes. The international enforcement of prohibition has made the illegal drug market the biggest business in the world. On the national or even international scale, it far exceeds the defense industry. Because these drugs are illegal, and therefore shipped secretly on the black market, some secretive agencies of the federal government are able to act covertly as a transportation link in the drug smuggling apparatus, an operation that brings huge multi-ton shipments of drugs into the United States undetected by our border agents.

Since one of these government agencies has a secret budget, the transportation expense, which is the major cost of the drug smuggling trade, is thereby absorbed into the budget of this and possibly other similar government agencies and subsequently paid for by the American taxpayer. This naturally allows the beneficiaries and recipients of such taxpayer largess to have a very unfair competitive advantage on the black market. We can see that the very richest members of organized crime, the wealthiest secret financiers of the drug market, receive major benefits from The War on Drugs and are able to fully exploit the prohibited status of these drugs at taxpayer expense.

Also, the armies of drug-producing countries like Colombia, Peru, Panama, Chile, Guatemala, Mexico, and in the past Haiti (and our friends the Contras), are armed and supplied with trucks and guns, bullets, and uniforms by the US taxpayer. Then these armies use this military equipment, supposedly supplied to them to fight the drug lords and their drug trade or communism, instead to transport and guard very large shipments of drugs from the production centers to the depots where it is shipped directly into the USA.

These armies, are also involved in massive human rights violations against their own people. These armies are used to terrorize the peasant farmers who grow the coca plants and poppies from which cocaine and heroin are produced. This is done to keep the price of the raw materials used to produce drugs at their lowest levels. So we see that when the American taxpayer supplies the uniforms, guns and trucks for these armies, we are helping these brutal armies to stay in power, independent of civilian control, and helping keep the profit for the local farmer down and increase the profit for the drug refining laboratories and the drug lords.

This pattern is now and has been occurring in every South and Central American government that the CIA has installed. The irony of this pervasive pattern should not be overlooked. We are all paying for it. We are also paying with our taxes for the planes that are used to fly these drugs into safe airports that are often in army or navy installations, and we are paying for the fuel that is used to fly these planes from their rendezvous, in the country of origin, to the safe military bases in the USA. What this means is that the most expensive part of the drug trade, which is the transportation expense, is being paid by the American taxpayer.

Since this black market is a cash business these taxpayer subsidies are going to support people who can afford to make inter-bank multi-million dollar money transfers without drawing notice to themselves because they are doing similar large denomination legal transfers on a regular, if not daily basis. That kind of transaction would surely be noticed if it happened infrequently. This means that some very rich elite and high placed persons, individuals who can afford to pay cash for tons of drugs, are being subsidized by working-class and middle-class people who are having a hard time making ends meet. These taxpayers think that their tax money is being used to fight drug importation. Instead the tax money that pours into these secret government agencies and these despotic foreign armies is being used to subsidize a huge segment of the illegal drug trade.

Then there is the exploding prison industry, the fastest growing industry in California and many other states in the USA, states with struggling economies. Half the people incarcerated in these overcrowded and expensive prison facilities are there for some kind of non-violent drug law violation. At this time that is a number somewhere in the vicinity of 1,500,000. It costs the American taxpayer more than 50 billion dollars to keep these non-violent people incarcerated for just one year.

There are also the side issues of lawyers, judges, and court costs, which also must be paid for either by taxes or personal income. This must amount to an additional sum of several billion dollars. Of course, there are all the law enforcement professionals and agencies whose job it is to enforce prohibition. These are good jobs with the best of benefits, such as health plans and retirement funds. Since no one knows the exact figure for the secret CIA budget, one must assume a multi-billion dollar figure. Some estimates have alluded to a 30 billion dollar figure. I would not be surprised if it was much higher than that.

Analysis of these aforementioned facts reveals some obvious conclusions. Prohibition, the War on Drugs, vastly benefits (1) organized crime the largest big-time drug financiers, (2) the drug lords who produce the refined product that is smuggled into the USA and other countries around the world, (3) the prison industry, (4) the law enforcement agencies charged with enforcing prohibition and waging the War on Drugs, (5) the upper levels of the drug distribution network, (6) corrupt politicians and appointed officials. The profits are so high that there is plenty of money to support all these illegal beneficiaries.

I am certain that if the sources of so-called soft money contributions to political campaigns could be known and analyzed, we would find that organized crime is the biggest and most generous "political action committee" in this country. The history of prohibition confirms this viewpoint. So let us again review the major beneficiaries of the War on Drugs. They are organized crime, the prison industry, corrupt South and Central American armies, the legal profession, corrupt politicians, and law enforcement agencies. Obviously, this includes a very small segment of the total U.S. population.

Now let's take a look at who is losing or being hurt by the War on Drugs. First and foremost there is the customers, the drug users. These include all from the casual or recreational users to the addicted drug abusers. Although it may not be true of the controlled casual or recreational user, every addict that I have ever known has been in some kind of pain, most usually psychological pain, unresolved from a troubled childhood. A society that breeds selfishness creates painful childhoods.

Our competitive society creates and rewards intense driving ambition and selfishness, along with stress and fear of others and punishes the poor with economic hardships. All these conditions make child rearing more difficult. Normally the place of employment is out of the house, and parenting is at best a part-time experience for most of us. We have grown used to generation after generation of latchkey children who grow up lonely, alienated, and in many cases, abused either psychologically or physically. From this pool of pain our addict population is recruited, not only from the lower classes, but from all levels of society.

Arresting and jailing these people only causes their pain to increase and intensifies their desire to seek some sort of relief. The stigma of prohibition, the court process, and imprisonment causes automatic denial and delays treatment or makes it financially impossible. By forcing addiction underground, we can hide from it, but we make the problem of addiction worse instead of better.

If our present prohibition policies were succeeding we would expect to see less addiction, but instead we have overcrowded our court system with more cases and our penal institutions with more inmates than at any time in our history. With the possible exceptions of Russia and China, we have more people in prison than any other country in the world. Clearly, if our stated goal is less drug use, our present prohibition policy is not working. One and one-half million citizens whose "pursuit of happiness", is made illegal by present laws are languishing in prison, rather than receiving treatment, living at home, working, and paying taxes.

To find, arrest, and prosecute these people, our law enforcement system is encouraged, trained, and even forced to violate the constitutional civil rights guaranteed to each and every citizen. We all can see the gradual erosion of our great Constitution and the Bill of Rights. With present prohibition policies, if the truth were known, half the citizens of the United States have NO constitutional protections at all.

So we are losing our freedom, our way of life, and are already halfway to a hidden agenda that has the eventual goal of creating a bankrupt, banana republic from this once-great nation. The "death squads", i.e. right-wing extremist so-called militia, are armed and in place, and if not for the costly error to themselves in the tragedy of Oklahoma City, things would be silently rolling right along, uninterrupted in this ultimate horrifying direction.

The practice of dealing with victimless crime by police violence and unconstitutional laws of enforcement for prohibited pursuits of happiness is so widespread that even the so-called militia can tell by the smell that something is not right with the Constitutional protections. Some say that the overreactions of law enforcement agencies in such extreme examples as the ATF/FBI Waco raid were inspired by what has become standard procedure in prohibition enforcement.

I am sure there is at least a grain of truth in viewpoint of the far-right militia. Complaints of this nature by large national organizations such as the NRA are not without example. Acting on false information obtained by deals with arrested offenders of prohibition laws have resulted in numerous deaths inflicted by over-excited drug enforcement agents. While at the same time, huge fortunes are being made, supported by a multi-billion dollars taxpayer subsidy.

These incidents are well documented; they are not the extremist conspiracy theories of gun lobbyists, or the manic militia. The systematic erosion of the Bill of Rights is part and parcel of the War on Drugs. Although tobacco and alcohol, the most dangerous drugs in common use today, cause over one-half million deaths in this country each year, they are legal ways to follow the Constitutionally protected right to the "pursuit of happiness".

Other, less harmful avenues of such pursuits are now prohibited. This is clearly unconstitutional, illogical, irrational, and manifestly unjust. When you count the citizens of our so-called free society who are presently imprisoned for non-violent drug offenses, somewhere close to one and one-half million, this is no small matter. This is not a question of some day, maybe, no, these are the people whose lives have already been ruined because their ways of pursuing happiness were found to be legally unacceptable.

There certainly is a constitutional conflict here. The problem of drug addiction, much of which is created by prohibition, is not a legal problem, and the only solution is a medical solution, both psychological and physical. Any other approach, as history and present events show, is doomed to failure. As we now see, the collateral damage from this failed social policy is just as dramatic as the direct damage.

Besides the constitutional crisis, there are the financial consequences. If you add up all the expenses, both of enforcement and the subsidized smuggling, the prisons and treatment expenses, you get a figure of very close to the yearly national deficit of 200 billion dollars, all of which is acting as a subsidy for organized crime at its highest and most well organized level.

This expense, which must be born by the taxpayer, is bankrupting our economy. There is no money left over for social programs. When these programs are removed it only increases the trauma of poverty and the desperation that goes with it. Crime (of necessity) increases, especially where vast differences in economic strata coincide. People will naturally resort to more and more risky behavior when faced with starvation while a rich and opulent environment exists just across the tracks.

This is not extremist theory. This is historical fact, proven over and over again since the beginning of recorded human history. Don't for one second think that the people who are framing the draconian cuts in social services are not also aware of this. They would have to be first-class idiots not to understand this truth. This truth is a big part of what the Old and New Testament are about.

So why are they doing it? My view is that they want an uncontrollable, violent, and crime ridden social condition, which brings with it the disintegration of our free society and the apparent need under those conditions for martial law, an outcome not too different from what the pundits are calling the paranoid delusions of the far-right, extremist militias. It's not, however, about guns, what it's really about is protecting the biggest business in the world, drug smuggling, and protecting it with continued prohibition.

Our courts are jammed, our jails are jammed. Violent offenders are let loose to keep nonviolent drug offenders in jail for cruel and unjustly long sentences. The costs keep rising every year and the jails are fuller and fuller, which proves beyond the shadow of a doubt that prohibition is not working to stop drug use in any meaningful way. To coin a plebeian phrase, "It's as plain as the nose on your face."

Okay, let's tally up the losers of the War on Drugs. The biggest losers are the average hard-working tax-paying citizens who are fooled into thinking this is a real and sincere effort to end the scourge of drug abuse. Those people lose along with everyone else who values living in a safe, free and peaceful society. The poor, disadvantaged, underclass will become an army of homeless, hopeless, needy, sick and dying people of all ages, on the streets in front of our eyes.

The sight of this human suffering will bring nothing but more desperation and more degradation. It will make today's problems look like a Sunday picnic. Remember economic decline and crime and violence have always throughout history gone hand-in-hand. Crimes of violence, usually headlined by wife beating and child abuse, are the pressures that disintegrate the family unit, and create more unwed mothers and more property crimes as well as murder, and are always multiplied by poverty.

Also, our justice system itself, from court to prison to parole, is already so constipated it has ceased to fulfill its basic function, to provide justice. Violent rapist kidnappers are released while nonviolent potheads are kept in jail in their place, and we continually hear politicians promising to build more and more jails. Eventually no matter how rich and prosperous our economy may seem to be now, this kind of policy will leave it in ruins. Moreover, it will be a ruin controlled by organized crime. Everyone but organized crime, the police, and the prison industry and the politicians they have bought, lose about everything we've ever had to be proud of or thankful for or to hope for in the future. There goes the "American Dream." Come on America wake up!! I'm not the only one with these frightening predictions but I am one of the few who can successfully "pin the tail on the donkey."

So who do you think is really in favor of this War on Drugs scam? Isn't it a bit of a stretch to imagine the people profiting from the drug trade black market to be in favor of legalization. It's hard to imagine someone voluntarily relinquishing a 3000 percent profit for just a 100 percent profit. On the other hand, if I, the trustee of a small portfolio of mostly mutual stocks, could realize a 100 percent profit on this investment I would be overjoyed, ecstatic. The overall effects of the War on Drugs are a mockery of our whole capitalistic free market economic system, and our free representative political system.

What is the answer? There are a number of approaches, but this is the one I like the best: Legalize drugs, but make everyone who wishes to buy potentially addictive drugs get a government identification prescription card authorizing purchase of just so much of this drug per month. Sell these drugs at the drugstore, and charge a government tax on them to fund treatment centers, thereby relieving the non-drug user of any tax burden for such services. If the individual becomes addicted, mandate treatment. If the addict refuses treatment, take back or invalidate the identification card.

We must realize that some addicts are going to need a series of treatments, but since these treatments are being paid for by drug taxes, eventually they will grow up and be cured. Give people free access to non-addictive substances such as peyote and marijuana. Standardize and regulate the production of drugs by the FDA so they are safer to use. Continue to ban potentially lethal drugs such as the elephant tranquilizer known as "angel dust." Tax tobacco and alcohol so that addiction to them can be treated and thereby reduce the huge medical expense that is draining our medical and economic system so severely.

With such a sane program of humane medical intervention, paid for by taxes on the sale of the drugs purchased by the addict, we could immediately start to see progress in our so-far unsuccessful effort to reduce the problem of drug addiction. We would, by making these drugs of superior quality available at drugstores at reasonable markups, remove the black market trade in them along with the business opportunity for the street dealer on up the ladder of the organized crime distribution network

By removing the legal stigma from the user we could finally determine the real dimensions of this social problem. We would remove the financial burden of treatment from the backs of the non-using taxpayer. We would automatically stop the slide down the slippery slope to police state fascism that we are now experiencing and finally we could balance the national budget in one or two years instead of seven.

We could perform this balancing act without removing the social safety net that keeps our society functional. We would end the cruel rule of the violent armies of South and Central America and thus remove the terror our once free Southern neighbors have had to live with. By doing this we would be ending the blatant displays of inhumanity these prohibition polices have fostered, both here and abroad. By so doing we can save our freedom and our free market system and advance the world towards the teachings of Jesus Christ: paradise on this earth, loving our neighbor, and helping those who need our help rather than hating them and inflicting even more severe pain on them.

By allowing, even helping Adolph Hitler come to power, we watched, whether we knew it or not, the destruction of Western European Judeo-Christian values and heritage. The earth is the "Garden of Paradise." The only thing that is wrong with it is what we human beings have done to it. I believe that we as a race, the human race, still have a chance to save ourselves and bring about this holy vision, but certainly not in the direction we are presently going. Because there are so many people here in our country unjustly languishing behind bars, subject to sub-human treatment and denied basic human needs, all because of unjust laws, the repeal of prohibition is the necessary first step in a new and positive direction. It promises to bring about our ageless striving to become one with the universe and nature (ourselves and our children) truly in the way the Lord intended. To do otherwise and continue in our present direction is tantamount to committing racial suicide. More than ever the choice is ours.

0-595-24700-8